ANNABEL KARMEL

Find out what this is on page 96

DK

A Dorling Kindersley Book

You Can COOK

LONDON, NEW YORK,
MELBOURNE, MUNICH, and DELHI

Designed by Rachael Foster
Edited by Penny Smith,
Lorrie Mack, Wendy Horobin, Fleur Star
Additional design by Rachael Smith,
Lauren Rosier
Photography Dave King
Food stylists Seiko Hatfield,
Martha Dunkerley

Recipe Consultant Caroline Stearns

Production editor Sean Daly
Production controller Jen Lockwood
Publishing manager Bridget Giles

First published in Great Britain in 2010 by
Dorling Kindersley Limited,
80 Strand, London, WC2R 0RL

Text copyright © 2010 Annabel Karmel
Layout and design copyright © 2010 Dorling
Kindersley Limited
A Penguin Company

4 6 8 10 9 7 5 3
014 – 175933 – March/2010

A CIP catalogue record for this book is available
from the British Library

ISBN: 978-1-40535-070-9

Colour reproduction by Alta Images, UK
Printed and bound in China

Discover more at
www.dk.com

Contents

About this book

One of the great pleasures in life is eating and if you can cook, you will always be able to conjure up a delicious meal even if you only have a few ingredients.

So I'm going to show you how easy it is to master basic cooking skills, prepare tasty meals, and have fun along the way.

One thing is for sure – everyone loves a good cook!

Bon appetit.

Annabel Karmel

Getting started

Look through this book and choose your recipe. Do you have everything you need? Check, and shop if you are missing anything. Then follow the tips below for safe, hygienic – and happy cooking!

Have fun cooking!

Kitchen safety

☆ Always tie back long hair and roll up loose sleeves so they don't get in the way.

☆ Use oven gloves when handling anything hot.

☆ Keep pan handles turned to the side – you don't want to knock the pans over.

☆ Mop up spills straight away so you don't slip on them.

☆ ALWAYS be especially careful when handling sharp knives or electrical equipment.

Kitchen hygiene

☆ The first thing to do when you start cooking is WASH YOUR HANDS!

☆ Cut up meat and vegetables on separate boards.

☆ Wash fruit and vegetables before you cook them.

☆ Store cooked and raw meat in separate compartments in the fridge.

☆ Wipe down surfaces and wash up when you finish cooking.

Reading the recipes

Symbols to look out for

 This tells you how long it takes to prepare a dish. It's just a guide – with practice, you get quicker at cooking.

 This tells you how long a dish takes to cook – on the hob as well as in the oven.

 This shows the number of servings for older children and adults. Younger children will eat less.

 All the recipes in this book are to be made under adult supervision. But when this symbol appears, extra care should be taken.

Weighing ingredients

It's a good idea to measure out ingredients before you start cooking – be sure to measure carefully!

Abbreviations

Metric measures
g = grams
ml = millilitres

Imperial measures
oz = ounces
lb = pounds
fl oz = fluid ounces

Spoon measures
tsp = teaspoon
tbsp = tablespoon
(Make these level.)

Kitchen equipment

Here's equipment you will find in lots of family kitchens. You'll need to use some of these items to make the recipes in this book.

Palette knife

Spaghetti claw

Basting brush

Mallet

Peelers

Sharp knife

Kitchen scissors

Garlic crusher

Whisks

Wooden spoon

Spatula

Baking paper

Kitchen foil

Muffin tin

Round cake tin

Baking tray

Square cake tin

Small bowls

Large bowl

Large saucepan

Crepe pan

Frying pan

Chopping boards

Grater

Electric mixer

Food blender

Spatulas

Rolling pin

Masher

Sieves

Bundt tin

Cooling rack

Small tart tins

Piping bag and nozzles

Cookie cutters

Wok

Griddle pan

Lemon squeezer

Colander

Loaf tin

Healthy eating

The key to a healthy diet is to eat lots of different kinds of food. This includes fresh fruit and vegetables, and protein-rich foods to help you grow. Eating cakes or biscuits as part of this diet is okay too – just don't eat them all the time, or instead of other foods.

The right stuff
Food is fuel for your body, giving you nutrients (vitamins and minerals) to keep you well. Eating a balanced diet of different kinds of foods is all part of being healthy.

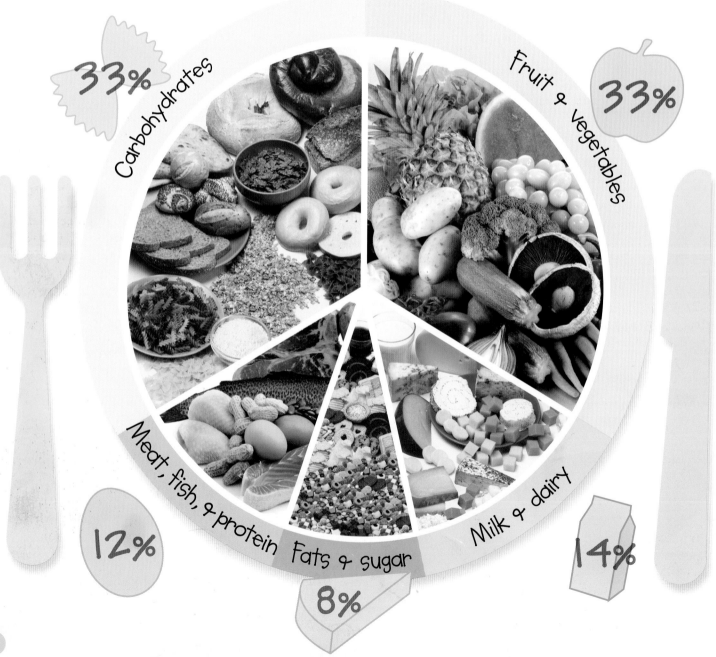

33% Carbohydrates

Fruit & vegetables 33%

Meat, fish, & protein 12%

Fats & sugar 8%

Milk & dairy 14%

A healthy balance

Every day, you should eat food from all of the five food groups. Each group has a different job to do, but it's important to get the balance right! Fill up on carbohydrates and fruit and vegetables, but don't eat too much fat and sugar.

Carbohydrates

Bread, potatoes, cereals, rice, and pasta give you energy to work and play. Wholegrain breads and cereals are higher in fibre and give longer lasting energy than white bread or refined cereals.

Fruit and vegetables

You should eat at least five portions of fruit and vegetables every day. Vegetables that are frozen within hours of being picked can be just as nutritious as fresh ones.

Milk and dairy

Dairy foods, such as milk and cheese, contain calcium. Your body needs this mineral to keep your bones, teeth, nails, and hair in good repair. Semi-skimmed and skimmed milk contain as much calcium as whole milk.

Meat, fish, and protein

You need protein to grow. It builds up your muscles and keeps you strong. Protein is found in meat, fish, chicken, eggs, and pulses (peas, beans, nuts, and lentils).

Fats and sugar

Your body needs some fat, but too much can make you ill. Butter, oil, cheese, and food made with these things (such as cakes) are fatty. Sugar provides a burst of energy, but too much is bad for your teeth.

Eat a rainbow of colour

You can get a good mix of vitamins and minerals by eating a variety of differently coloured fruit and vegetables. The more colourful the fruit, the better it is for you as the colour contains antioxidants that help protect us against disease. So a red grapefruit is better for you than an ordinary white grapefruit.

> ☆ Annabel's healthy eating tips
> ☆ *Always eat breakfast*
> ☆ *Eat fruit and or vegetables with every meal*
> ☆ *If you need a snack, eat fruit rather than sweets*
> ☆ *Eat fish at least twice a week*

How much should I eat?

Healthy eating is not just about what you eat, but how much too. If you feel uncomfortably full, you've probably eaten too much! It is a lot more comfortable to eat several smaller meals throughout the day.

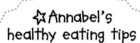
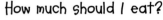

Did you know your body is made up of 70% water?

Junk food

Food that contains a lot of sugar or fat is called "junk food". It's okay to eat this occasionally, but only as part of a balanced diet. There are some healthier versions in this book that you can make yourself.

Know your fruit

Fruit is not only juicy and scrumptious –
it keeps you healthy and helps you
grow strong! Try to eat at least
five portions of fruit (or vegetables)
every day.

I've used all this lovely fruit in the recipes that follow.

Banana

Apples

Pear

Pineapple

Papaya

Mango

Dried fruit

Dried apricots

Dried cranberries

Raisins

Dried mango

Desiccated coconut

Sultanas

Orange

Lemon

Lime

Grapes

Kiwi

Strawberries

Blackberries

Plums

Blueberries

Raspberries

11

Know your vegetables

Most vegetables are bright, crunchy, and full of flavour and they're *very* good for you. Here are the ones you'll use in recipes in this book.

Parsnip

Sweetcorn

Potatoes

Onion

Carrots

Broccoli

Red onion

Leek

Garlic

Shallots

Spinach

Courgette

Butternut squash

Salad stuff

Iceberg lettuce

Little gem lettuce

Spring onions

Celery

Rocket leaves

Peppers

Chilli peppers

Tomatoes

French beans

Watercress

Mangetout

Peas

Bean sprouts

Avocado

First steps

In this chapter you'll learn the basics of cooking, like how to make fluffy scrambled eggs or an omelette. And breakfast will never be dull when you can make perfect pancakes or a heart-shaped fried egg in the middle of a slice of toast. There are some wonderful creative ideas for sandwiches and wraps. And for dessert there are fabulous ways with fruit, from a tropical fruit salad to my indulgent frozen berries with chocolate sauce. So tuck in and enjoy the fruits of your labour...

15

All about EGGS

Boiled eggs

The secret to perfect boiled eggs isn't really a secret at all – it's just timing! The longer you cook an egg, the harder it will be.

Eggs are one of the most useful foods we have.

They are fantastic cooked by themselves as a delicious breakfast or light meal, and they are an essential ingredient in lots of recipes from omelettes and pancakes to biscuits and cakes. Eggs are packed with protein so they help you grow and stay healthy. Most of the eggs we eat come from chickens.

What's inside an egg?

When you crack open an egg, you'll find the white and the yolk. Although supermarket eggs can't turn into chicks, some other eggs can, and the white and yolk are what the growing chick feeds on.

Brown or white eggs?

You might like one colour more than the other, but inside they are just the same. The colour comes from the breed of chicken that lays them. Hens that lay brown eggs tend to be bigger than hens that lay white eggs.

Is your egg fresh?

To find out, put it in a bowl of water. If it sinks, it's fresh. But if it floats, it probably isn't – so don't eat it!

Anyone for an egg?

How do you like your egg?

☆Annabel's Tip
To help stop an egg cracking when you put it in boiling water, warm it in hot tap water first.

To boil an egg, fill a saucepan with water and bring it to a full boil over high heat.

Lower the egg into the boiling water.

Simmer for **6 minutes** for medium-firm yolks.

A hard-boiled egg...

.. takes 12 minutes. When it's done, drop it into cold water to prevent a grey ring forming around the yolk.

Simmer for **4 minutes** for soft, runny yolks.

Simmer for **8 minutes** for firm yolks.

Scrambled eggs

Cook beaten eggs over a low heat, and serve them when they're still soft and moist.

Whisk together the eggs, milk, salt and pepper.

You will need: 2 eggs, 1 tbsp milk, salt and pepper, a knob of butter.

Melt half the butter in a pan. Add the egg mixture and stir constantly while the eggs are cooking. When they start to thicken, stir in the rest of the butter and serve immediately.

You will need:

2 eggs
salt and pepper
a knob of butter

Basic omelette

Here's how you make a delicious basic omelette. Serve it plain, try one of my filling suggestions (below), or invent your own!

Whisk

1 Break the eggs into a bowl and whisk them until they're slightly frothy. Season with salt and pepper.

2 Heat a small frying pan – about 14 cm (5 ½ in) – over a medium heat. Melt the butter and when it starts to foam, tip in the eggs.

3 Stir the eggs once or twice, then leave them to cook undisturbed for about 30 seconds.

Lift

4 When the eggs start to set at the edge of the pan, lift the cooked edge towards the centre. At the same time, tip the pan so the uncooked egg runs into the space that's left. Do this 3 or 4 times until there is no runny egg left on the surface of the omelette.

Omelette fillings

• 30 g (1 oz) ham, cut into strips, with slices of tomato

• 30 g (1 oz) grated hard cheese such as Cheddar or Gruyère

• 30 g (1 oz) smoked salmon, cut into thin strips

• 1 tsp chopped soft herbs – try parsley with dill, chervil, or chives

• 1 tbsp each sweetcorn and diced red pepper, plus one thinly sliced spring onion

• a handful of button mushrooms sautéed in a knob of butter

Fold

5 Now add your filling. Here, we're using a handful of fresh parsley, sprinkled all over the eggs. Or, if you like, whisk your herbs into the eggs at step 1.

6 Turn off the heat and fold the omelette over. Transfer it to a plate and serve immediately.

Eat up while it's still hot!

How to make toast

It's easy to make toast in a toaster, but just as nice when you use a grill. Lay your bread on the grill pan, then put it close to the heat – it takes only a couple of minutes for one side to turn golden. When it does, turn the bread over and toast the other side.

☆Annabel's Tip

Once the toast is made, let it stand for a minute or two. This lets the steam escape so the toast doesn't get soggy.

Now you can treat yourself to my tasty toast toppers

Tomato and cheese

You will need: butter, 1 slice toast, 1 sliced tomato, pepper 40 g (1½ oz) grated hard cheese such as Cheddar

Ready to grill

Done!

Sprinkle with a little chopped parsley.

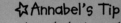

1 Heat the grill to high. Spread a little butter on the toast and lay thin slices of tomato on this. Let the tomato overhang the crust to stop the crust burning. Season with pepper, then scatter over the cheese.

2 Grill for 1½ to 2 minutes until the cheese is bubbling and turning brown. It will be hot! So let it cool a little before you eat it.

Hearty egg

You will need: 2 tsp oil, 1 lightly toasted slice of bread, 1 egg, salt and pepper

You can eat this piece too!

Use a pastry cutter to make a hole in your toast.

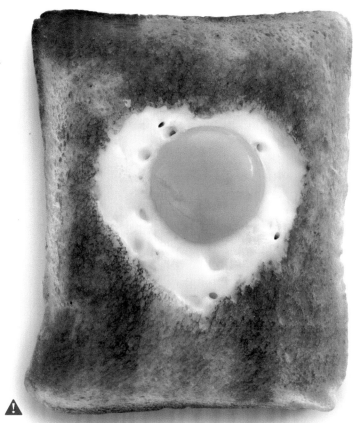

Heat the oil in a small frying pan. Cut a hole in the middle of the toast. Break the egg into a cup. Put the toast in the frying pan and gently slide the egg into the hole. Add a little salt and pepper. Turn the heat to low and cook for about 4 minutes until the egg white has set. Then serve.

Here are some savoury toasties — over the page, there are sweet ones

Grilled garlic toast

You will need: 30 g (1 oz) softened butter, 1 small clove crushed garlic, 2 tbsp grated Parmesan cheese, pepper, 4 slices toasted baguette

1 Heat the grill to high. Mix together the butter, garlic, Parmesan, and a grinding of pepper. Spread the butter mixture generously on the toast.

Sprinkle with chopped parsley

2 Grill for about 30 seconds until melted. Sprinkle with parsley and serve immediately.

21

Caramelized bananas

You will need: butter, 1 slice toast, 1 sliced banana, ½ tbsp soft light brown sugar, pinch of cinnamon

1 Preheat the grill to high. Lightly butter the toast and lay the banana on top. Mix together the sugar and cinnamon and sprinkle over the banana.

2 Grill for 1 or 2 minutes until the sugar is bubbling and golden. Watch carefully so it doesn't burn. Cool slightly before serving.

Try some sweet toppings on your toast too. Fruit is perfect!

Grilled peaches and honey

You will need: butter, 1 slice toast, 1 sliced peach, 1 tbsp mascarpone cheese, 1 tsp honey,

This is extra tasty served on brioche

Serve while still warm

1 Preheat the grill to medium. Lightly butter the toast and lay the peach slices on top.

2 Grill gently until the peach softens, then add the mascarpone cheese and drizzle over the honey.

Real hot chocolate

Once you've had hot chocolate made with *real* chocolate, you'll never want any other kind!

☆ **Annabel's Tip**
For even more of a treat, top your hot chocolate with whipped cream, a dusting of cocoa, or a sprinkling of shaved chocolate.

Try it with milk chocolate instead

frothy top

1 Put the milk in a pan and gently bring to the boil.

2 Put the chocolate, vanilla, and sugar into a heatproof jug.

3 Pour the hot milk onto the chocolate and whisk until the chocolate has melted. Serve while it's still frothy on top.

Find out how to make these ginger biscuits on page 106.

23

First pancakes

These simple pancakes are sometimes called "crepes". The first one you make may be a bit messy as the pan's still warming up – think of it as the cook's treat!

You will need:

110 g (4 oz) plain flour
pinch of salt
1 egg
300 ml (10 fl oz) milk
15 g (½ oz) butter, melted
sunflower oil, for greasing

1 Put the flour and salt in a large bowl. Make a well in the centre, then add the egg and half the milk.

2 Whisk into a thick, smooth batter. Then whisk in the rest of the milk and melted butter. Or just whizz everything in a blender.

3 Heat a non-stick frying pan – about 20 cm (8 in) – on medium heat. Lightly grease the pan with oil. Pour in 3 tbsp batter. Tilt the pan so the batter covers the base.

4 Cook for 1 to 1½ minutes until golden brown underneath. Then flip the pancake with a spatula (or toss if you dare!) and cook for a further minute.

Serve with sugar and lemon

☆**Annabel's Tip**
To serve the pancakes all at once, stack them on a plate with baking parchment in between each one, and keep them warm in a low oven.

American pancakes

Pancakes are a great way to start the day, since they give you lots of energy. As these are quite small, you should be able to cook two or three at one time.

You will need:

150 g (5½ oz) plain flour
2 tbsp granulated sugar
½ tsp bicarbonate of soda
1 tsp baking powder
large pinch of salt
250 ml (8 fl oz) buttermilk
1 egg
¼ tsp vanilla extract
200 g (7 oz) blueberries
sunflower oil, for greasing
2 tbsp maple syrup

1 Put the flour, sugar, bicarbonate of soda, baking powder, and salt in a bowl. Add half the buttermilk, the egg, and vanilla extract.

2 Whisk everything together to make a batter. Add the remaining buttermilk and whisk until smooth.

3 Add the blueberries and mix them into the batter gently. Try not to squash them.

4 Lightly oil and heat a non-stick frying pan. Drop in 2 tbsp batter per pancake. Cook for 1½ to 2 minutes until golden underneath and bubbling on top. Flip over and cook for a further 1 to 2 minutes. Serve with maple syrup.

For extra flavour, serve with a knob of butter

☆ **Annabel's Tip**
You don't have to use buttermilk in this recipe. Instead, mix together 110 g (4 oz) plain yoghurt and 110 ml (4 fl oz) skimmed milk.

All sorts of sandwiches

A sandwich is just two slices of bread with filling inside. But there are zillions of variations – different fillings... different breads... toasted or plain... Here are a few ideas.

First choose your bread

Making a club sandwich

Spread mayonnaise on a slice of toast. Add a layer of cranberry sauce.

Add half the sliced cooked chicken, and scatter over half the crispy bacon.

Chicken club sandwich

To prepare your ingredients, toast 3 slices of bread, slice a cooked, skinless, chicken breast, grill 2 rashers of streaky bacon, slice 1 tomato, and shred 2 lettuce leaves. Then follow the steps (right) to put the sandwich together.

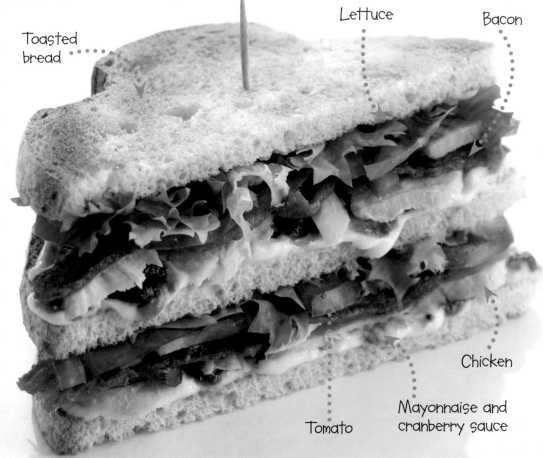

Toasted bread

Lettuce

Bacon

Chicken

Tomato

Mayonnaise and cranberry sauce

Add half the sliced tomato and shredded lettuce, salt and pepper.

Put another layer of toast on top. Then repeat the steps above.

26

Ham with honey-mustard mayonnaise

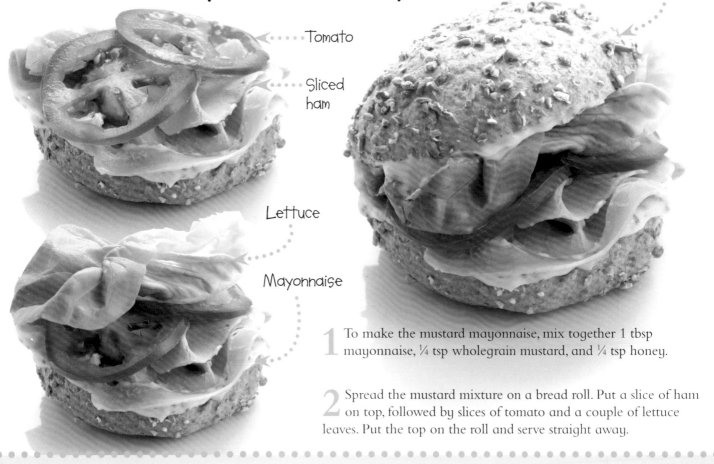

Tomato

Sliced ham

Seedy roll

Lettuce

Mayonnaise

1 To make the mustard mayonnaise, mix together 1 tbsp mayonnaise, ¼ tsp wholegrain mustard, and ¼ tsp honey.

2 Spread the mustard mixture on a bread roll. Put a slice of ham on top, followed by slices of tomato and a couple of lettuce leaves. Put the top on the roll and serve straight away.

Ricotta and roasted vegetables

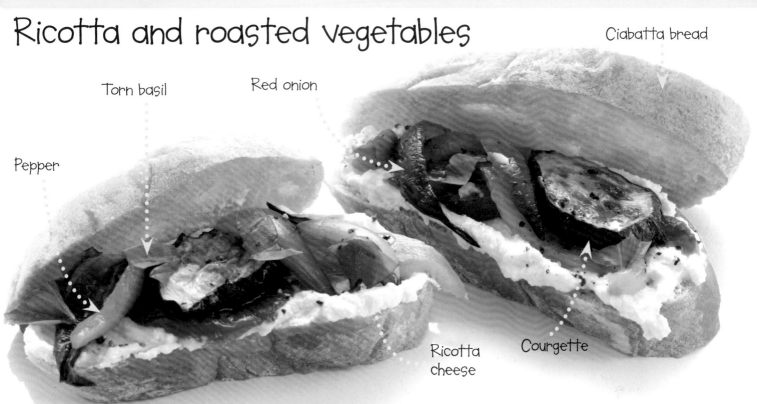

Torn basil

Red onion

Ciabatta bread

Pepper

Ricotta cheese

Courgette

1 To roast the vegetables, put slices of red onion, courgette, and red and yellow pepper on a baking tray. Drizzle with olive oil and roast at 200°C/400°F/Gas 6 for 20 minutes.

2 Spread a layer of ricotta cheese over a slice of ciabatta bread. Scatter on the roasted vegetables and a few torn basil leaves. Season with pepper and serve.

Open sandwiches

Egg, cheese, and chive

Cress

Hardboiled egg

Baguette

Yoghurt and chive dressing

Grated cheese

To make the yoghurt dressing, mix together 1 tbsp Greek yoghurt, 1 tbsp mayonnaise, ½ tsp lemon juice, and 1 tsp snipped chives. Spread the mixture over the baguette. Then add grated Cheddar cheese, sliced hardboiled egg, and cress.

Prawn and watercress

Watercress

Prawns
Use either fresh or frozen prawns in this sandwich. Drain them first on kitchen paper.

Prawn in dressing

Slice of lemon

Ciabatta

To make the dressing, mix together 1 tsp mayonnaise, ¾ tsp lemon juice, salt and pepper. Gently stir in 85 g (3 oz) cooked prawns. Lightly butter the ciabatta (or use a baguette). Put a handful of watercress on top, then the dressed prawns. Garnish with lemon.

Wraps

Tomato, mozzarella, and pesto

⚠️ Warm the wrap in a dry frying pan. Spread over the pesto and mayonnaise mixture, then lay the mozzarella and tomato down the centre of the wrap. Season with salt and pepper and roll up.

☆ **Annabel's Tip**
To make your wraps easier to serve, fasten them closed with a cocktail stick.

Tortilla wrap

1 tbsp mayonnaise mixed with 1 tsp pesto

1 large tomato, skinned, deseeded, and quartered

60 g (2 oz) sliced mozzarella

Chicken Reuben

⚠️ Warm the wrap in a dry frying pan. Mix the mayonnaise with 2 to 3 drops lemon juice and ½ tbsp tomato ketchup (or just squirt on the ketchup) and spread over the wrap. Then scatter lettuce over half the wrap and layer the chicken and tomatoes on top. Add salt and pepper and roll up.

Roll up and eat!

Shredded lettuce

Tortilla wrap

30 g (1 oz) cooked chicken

3 cherry tomatoes

1 tbsp mayonnaise

Lemon

½ tbsp tomato ketchup

Cooking vegetables

Vegetables are a great way to add colour, texture, and healthy vitamins to a meal. Roast, boil, steam or stir-fry your favourites.

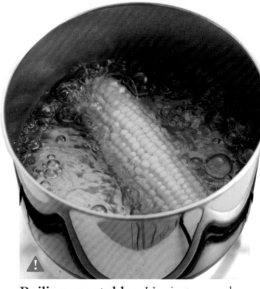

Steam

Boiling vegetables Use just enough water (slightly salted) to cover the vegetables. Bring to the boil, add the vegetables and cook until just soft but still a bit firm.

Steaming vegetables Cover the bottom of a pan with water. Add a steaming basket and bring the water to the boil. Then add your vegetables and put the lid on the pan. The vegetables hold on to most of their nutrients as they cook in the steam.

Roasted parsnip chips

2 Line a baking sheet with baking parchment. Lay the sliced parsnips on this. Sprinkle with olive oil and season with salt and pepper.

Roast

1 Preheat the oven to 180°C/350°F/Gas mark 4. Peel the parsnips and cut off the ends. Then cut the parsnips into thin slices – make them all about the same size.

Stir-fried vegetables with...   ... sweet chilli

For the sauce
1½ tbsp soy sauce
1 to 2 tsp sweet chilli sauce
(or to taste)

You will need:

85 g (3 oz) mangetout
1 large carrot
½ red pepper
85 g (3 oz) broccoli
1 tbsp sunflower oil
½ tsp grated ginger
60 g (2 oz) beansprouts
2 spring onions, thinly sliced

1 Cut the mangetout, carrot, and pepper into matchstick-sized pieces. Cut the broccoli into bite-sized florets.

2 Heat the sunflower oil in a wok or large frying pan over a high heat. Add the ginger and let it sizzle for 10 seconds, then add the carrots, pepper, and broccoli and stir-fry for 2 minutes.

3 Add the beansprouts and mangetout and stir-fry for one minute. Stir in the spring onions, then remove from the heat and stir in the soy sauce and the sweet chilli sauce. Serve immediately.

3 Roast for 15 minutes. Then turn the slices over and roast for 10 minutes. Turn them again and roast for a final 5 to 10 minutes until golden.

Fruit glorious fruit!

There are lots of yummy ways to eat fruit, whether it's fresh, frozen, or cooked.

Tropical fruit salad

You will need:

For the sauce

1 small ripe mango
3 tbsp tropical fruit juice
1 tbsp lime juice
1 tbsp icing sugar

For the salad

½ fresh pineapple
2 oranges
1 papaya
2 small bananas

1 To make the sauce, peel and slice the mango. Push it through a sieve, then mix it with the tropical fruit juice, lime juice, and sugar. Or simply whizz the sauce ingredients together in a blender.

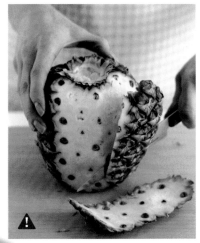

2 For the salad, peel and core the pineapple. Cut the fruit into cubes.

3 Peel the oranges and cut into segments. Cube the papaya, then peel and slice the bananas. Mix the fruit and add the sauce.

Serve with a glacé cherry

Frozen berries

You will need:

300 g (10 oz) fresh berries
(like blackberries, raspberries,
blueberries, and strawberries)
110 g (4 oz) white chocolate,
chopped into small pieces
150 ml (5½ fl oz) double cream

1 Freeze the berries on a baking sheet lined with parchment. Divide them between 4 bowls. Let them defrost until semi-frozen.

2 Put the white chocolate into a jug. Warm the double cream until it is hot but not boiling. Pour the hot cream over the white chocolate and stir until melted.

Pour on the sauce and serve immediately

Pear and plum crumble

Make 6 little crumbles, or one big one

You will need:

450 g (1 lb) pears, cored and cut into
chunks
450 g (1 lb) plums, stoned, quartered
60 g (2 oz) caster sugar

For the crumble topping
110 g (4 oz) plain flour
60 g (2 oz) wholemeal flour
½ tsp salt
85 g (3 oz) butter
60 g (2 oz) porridge oats
1 tsp ground ginger
110 g (4 oz) demerara sugar

1 Preheat the oven to 200°C/400°F/ Gas mark 6. Put the pears and plums into 6 heatproof dishes. Sprinkle on the caster sugar.

2 Put the flour and salt in a bowl. Rub in the butter. Then stir in the oats, ginger, and sugar. Sprinkle the topping on the fruit. Cook small crumbles for 30 minutes, and one large one for 40 to 45 minutes.

☆**Annabel's Tip**
*The crumble is cooked when it's golden
on top and bubbling at the sides.*

33

Light bites

When you're feeling a bit hungry it's good to have healthy foods on hand. Try making delicious soup like my sweetcorn chowder, fill baked potatoes with tempting toppings, or design your own fabulous fruit smoothies. And there are delicious salads here too. Not only will they make a tasty light meal – they are also a nice change from sandwiches in your lunchbox...

Sweetcorn chowder

A chowder is a lusciously thick and warming soup, usually made with potato. Use this recipe to make either a vegetarian or a chicken version.

You will need:

1 medium onion

1 small clove garlic

2 medium potatoes

15 g (½ oz) butter

750 ml (24 fl oz) vegetable stock

100 ml (3½ fl oz) milk

200 g (7 oz) tinned sweetcorn, drained

6 tbsp double or whipping cream

1 Chop the onion finely, crush the garlic, and peel and cut the potatoes into small cubes.

2 Melt the butter in a large saucepan. Cook the onion and garlic very gently for 10 to 12 minutes until soft.

3 Add the potato cubes, stock, and milk. Bring the mixture to the boil, then reduce the heat and simmer, partly covered, for 15 minutes.

4 Add the sweetcorn and simmer (partly covered again) for 5 to 10 minutes more until the potato is soft. If the mixture feels very thick, add 2 to 3 tbsp hot water.

Chicken chowder

To make this version, use chicken stock and add 100 g (3½ oz) shredded cooked chicken when you get to step 6.

5 Turn off the heat. Leave the mixture to cool, then put half aside in a bowl. If you have a hand blender, blend the remaining half in the saucepan until smooth. (Otherwise, blend it in a liquidizer, and return it to the saucepan.)

6 Add the soup in the bowl to the soup in the saucepan and stir in the cream. Reheat gently to serve.

Sprinkle on dill for flavour and colour

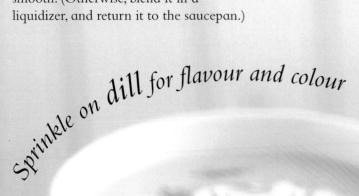

✿ *Annabel's Tip*
Americans like to serve chowder with crumbled saltine crackers. Similar types like cream crackers work just as well — or try lovely crusty bread (see page 44).

You will need:

2 boneless chicken breasts
2 red peppers
140 g (5 oz) fusilli pasta
olive oil, to brush the griddle
60 g (2 oz) rocket

For the marinade

2 tbsp olive oil
2 tsp lemon juice
1 clove garlic, crushed
salt and pepper

For the dressing

4 tbsp light olive oil
3 tbsp rice-wine vinegar
1½ tsp Dijon mustard
1 tbsp green pesto
2 tbsp snipped chives
2 tbsp chopped parsley

Chicken pasta salad with roasted peppers

To make this dish, you bash chicken with a mallet, peel peppers, and mix up a herby dressing. I've cooked my chicken on a griddle to make it stripy, but an ordinary frying pan is fine.

Lemony marinated chicken

Sweet roasted peppers

Time saver
Marinating the chicken gives it a fresh lemony flavour. But if you don't have time, you can leave out this step. The dish isn't the same, but it's still very tasty!

Bash

Marinate

1 Preheat the oven to 200°C/400°F/ Gas mark 6. Cover the chicken with clingfilm. Then bash it a few times with a mallet to flatten it.

2 For the marinade, mix up the oil, lemon juice, garlic, salt and pepper. Pour it over the chicken and leave for at least 20 minutes.

3 Cut the red peppers in half and take out the seeds and pith. Roast the peppers in the oven for 20 minutes until soft with blackened skins.

4 Put the peppers in a bowl. Cover with clingfilm and leave to cool. Peel off the skins and slice the flesh into thin strips.

5 Cook the pasta in boiling water according to the packet instructions. Drain, then rinse the pasta in cold water.

6 To cook the chicken, brush a griddle or frying pan with a little oil and heat it up. Cook the chicken for 4 minutes each side or until done.

Mix

7 To make the dressing, mix together the oil, vinegar, mustard, pesto, chives, and parsley.

8 When the chicken is cool enough to handle, cut it into bite-sized strips.

9 Put the chicken in a bowl with the peppers, pasta, and rocket. Add the dressing and mix everything together with your (very clean) hands. Serve.

You will need:

2 eggs
60 g (2 oz) Cheddar cheese
60 g (2 oz) skinless chicken breast, cooked
1 large tomato
1 small avocado
1 small little gem lettuce or
½ heart of romaine lettuce
3 tbsp mayonnaise
2 tbsp milk
½ tsp red-wine vinegar
¼ tsp Dijon mustard
2 to 3 drops Worcestershire sauce
salt and pepper

Cobb salad

An American invention, this tasty salad is made with avocado, hard-boiled eggs, and chicken. Serve it with fresh crusty bread for supper.

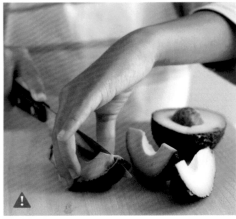

1 Bring a saucepan of water to the boil. Lower the eggs into the water and simmer for 12 minutes.

2 Transfer the eggs to a bowl of iced water (or run cold water over them). When cool, peel off the shells. Cut each egg into 4 lengthways. Dice the cheese and chicken into very small cubes. Cut the tomato into eight.

3 Slice the avocado and remove the skin. Then arrange the lettuce, avocado, egg, tomato, chicken, and cheese in a bowl.

Make the dressing

For the dressing, whisk together the mayonnaise, milk, vinegar, mustard, Worcestershire sauce, salt and pepper and serve with the salad.

Sprinkle with parsley

Layered salad

This colourful striped salad looks fantastic tipped out like a jelly.

You will need:

110 g (4 oz) small pasta shells
4 tbsp light mayonnaise
3 tbsp half-fat crème fraiche
2 tbsp tomato ketchup
2 tsp lemon juice
250 g (8 oz) small cooked prawns, drained and dried
2 tbsp chopped parsley
salt and pepper
1 x 198 g (7 oz) tin sweetcorn
1 large carrot, peeled and grated
1 bunch spring onions, finely sliced
¼ iceberg lettuce, sliced

1 Cook the pasta according to the packet instructions, then drain. Cool under cold running water. In a bowl, mix together the mayonnaise, crème fraiche, ketchup, lemon juice, prawns, parsley, and salt and pepper.

2 Line a 1.1 litre (2 pt) bowl with clingfilm. Spoon ½ the prawn mixture into the base. Put the pasta on top. Then sprinkle on the drained sweetcorn. Lay the grated carrot on this. Then add the remaining prawns, spring onions, and lettuce. Press down firmly. Chill in the fridge for 1 hour.

3 Just before serving, pop the salad into the freezer for 10 minutes. Then put a plate on top of the salad. Hold tight, and turn bowl and plate over to turn out the salad.

Flip over to turn out

Half the prawns

Pasta

Corn

Carrot

Half the prawns

Spring onions and lettuce

Add a twist of lemon and sprig of parsley

41

Making bread dough

It only takes a little effort and a few simple ingredients to make bread dough that's perfect for delicious small loaves, rolls, speciality breads – and pizza!

1 Put 60 ml (2 fl oz) of the warm (hand-hot) water in a small bowl with the sugar. Stir in the yeast and leave to stand for 10 minutes.

The yeast should start to froth. Frothy yeast looks like this.

2 Stir together the salt and flour in a large bowl. Make a well in the centre and pour in the melted butter and frothing yeast.

6 Transfer to a lightly oiled bowl, cover with clingfilm, and leave in a warm place for 1 hour to prove (double in size).

When the dough has doubled in size, it looks like this.

7 Knock the dough back – this means using your fists to squash out the air, then kneading it some more.

You will need:

300 ml (10 fl oz) warm water
1 tbsp sugar
1 x 7 g (¼ oz) sachet dried yeast
1 tsp salt

450 g (1 lb) strong white bread flour, plus extra for dusting
15 g (½ oz) melted butter
sunflower oil, for greasing
1 egg, beaten

Kneaded enough?
Poke a finger into the dough – if it's ready, it will spring back.

3 Rinse out the yeast bowl with 200 ml (7 fl oz) of the water and add to the flour. Mix to make a soft dough, adding more water as needed.

4 In the bowl, start forming the dough into a ball shape, ready to knead. Dust your work surface with flour to stop the dough from sticking.

5 Knead the dough for 10 minutes – use the heel of your hands to squash it away from you. Fold over the top end, turn it, and repeat.

8 We wanted to make 2 small loaves, so we divided the dough into 2 pieces. (See over the page for lots of other ideas.)

9 Put each piece in a greased 450 g (1 lb) loaf tin. Cover with oiled clingfilm and leave to prove again – for about 20 minutes this time, or until doubled in size.

10 While the bread is proving, preheat oven to 200°C/400°F/ Gas 6. Brush the loaves with beaten egg. Bake for 25 to 35 minutes until golden on top and hollow-sounding underneath.

43

What to make with your dough

To make bread rolls

Divide the dough in half, then half again and keep going until you have 16 pieces. Make into round shapes, then put on greased or lined baking sheets. Cover with oiled clingfilm and leave to prove in a warm place for 20 minutes or until doubled in size. Brush with beaten egg and decorate with seeds. Then bake in the oven for 15 to 20 minutes.

2 cottage loaves...

...or 16 small rolls

To decorate bread rolls

Plain rolls are delicious, but it's fun choosing different toppings too. Try grated Parmesan cheese, or sunflower, poppy, and sesame seeds.

Cottage loaves

Divide the dough equally into two. Then divide each piece into two again, but this time make one piece twice as big as the other. Shape them into rounds. Put the large rounds on an oiled baking sheet, with the small rounds on top. Push the floured handle of a wooden spoon through the middle of each loaf to join the two parts together. Brush the tops with beaten egg before baking.

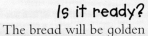

...or 2 small loaves...

Freezing bread

After the first prove, knock back the dough and shape it into rolls. Freeze on a baking sheet lined with clingfilm. Then transfer to resealable bags and store in the freezer. Leave in a warm place to defrost and prove, then cook as before.

Is it ready?

The bread will be golden brown when it's done. And when you tap the base with your hand, it will sound hollow.

...or 2 pieces of focaccia

Focaccia

Shape your dough into two flatish rectangles and leave to prove for 20 minutes. Brush with olive oil and sprinkle with sea salt. Then poke in pieces of rosemary. Cook the focaccia for 20 minutes or until golden on top with a hollow-sounding base.

Perfect baked potatoes

Jacket potatoes are the easiest meal ever – just put them in the oven and leave them to cook. All the recipes here are for four medium potatoes.

1 Preheat the oven to 200°C/400°F/Gas mark 6. Wash and dry the potatoes and rub oil all over their skins. Prick them with a fork so the moisture inside can escape as steam during cooking.

2 Put the potatoes on a baking sheet and bake them for 1 to 1½ hours. They are ready when the skins are crisp and the flesh is soft inside (push a fork in to check).

Cut a cross in the top of each potato and serve with butter and a little salt...

... or try my tasty filling ideas

Melting butter

☆Annabel's Tip
Choose potatoes that are firm and quite heavy. Cut out any blemishes or green parts before you cook them.

Cheese and squash filling

Peel, deseed, and slice ½ large butternut squash. Bake for 40 minutes with the potato. Scoop out the cooked potato and squash and mash together with 150 g (5½ oz) grated Cheddar cheese, 130 ml (4½ fl oz) crème fraiche, salt and pepper. Put back into the skins.

Tuna topping

Mix 185 g (6½ oz) tinned tuna with 2 sliced spring onions, 4 tbsp crème fraiche, 1 tbsp milk, 1 tsp lemon juice, 4 drops Worcestershire sauce, and 4 tbsp sweetcorn. Spoon onto 4 potatoes and top with 110 g (4 oz) grated Cheddar cheese.

Sprinkle with Parmesan cheese…

Grill until golden, then serve

…and bake for a further 15 minutes

Crispy bacon potatoes

Grill 8 bacon rashers until crisp. Blot on kitchen paper. Scoop out the cooked potato and mash with 130 ml (4½ fl oz) soured cream, 30 g (1 oz) butter, and 2 tbsp milk. Stir in 1 tsp snipped chives, salt and pepper. Spoon back into the potato skins and crumble the bacon over the top.

Heat through in the oven before serving

Crispy bacon

Snipped chives

Quick dips

Raspberry sauce

Whizz two handfuls of raspberries and a teaspoon of raspberry jam in a blender. Sieve to remove seeds.

Dip pear and mango in the sauce ⚠

Guacamole and tomato salsa

For the guacamole mash an avocado with the juice of ½ a lime, 1 tbsp of Greek yoghurt, salt and pepper. Stir in your choice of a finely chopped spring onion, a chopped tomato, or 1 to 2 tsp of chopped coriander.

Serve with tortilla chips or vegetable sticks ⚠

For the tomato salsa put 300 g (10 oz) halved tomatoes in a food processor with 4 chopped spring onions, ¼ red pepper, ¼ red chilli, and salt and pepper. Whizz for about 30 seconds.

Cottage-cheese dip

Chill and serve with fresh vegetables

Whizz 250 g (8 oz) cottage cheese with 3 tbsp mayonnaise, 2 tbsp ketchup, ¼ tsp lemon juice, 3 drops Worcester sauce. ⚠

Yoghurt dip with dulche de leche

Dip in your favourite fruit

Swirl a teaspoon of dulche de leche through a big dollop of Greek yoghurt and serve with pieces of fresh fruit.

Perfect popcorn

Warm, freshly popped corn is a delicious treat tossed in a little melted butter and a sprinkling of salt. Or try my special sweet variation.

You will need:
1 tbsp sunflower oil
110 g (4 oz) popping corn

1 Heat the oil in a large heavy-based pan. When the oil is shimmering, add the corn. Put on the lid tightly.

2 Let the corn pop for a minute or two until the popping starts to subside. Then shake the pan and let the corn pop again. Repeat until all the corn has popped.

Popcorn crunch

Melt 60 g (2 oz) butter, 110 g (4 oz) brown sugar, 2 tbsp golden syrup, and a pinch of salt in a pan. Mix with your cooked popcorn. Spread out on a baking sheet and bake for 25 to 30 minutes at 150°C/300°F/Gas 2. Stir halfway through.

Popped and ready to eat

Unpopped kernels

49

Fruit smoothies

Good colours, good flavours, good for you!
And these smoothies are so easy to make –
all you do is whizz up a few ingredients.
For extra-thick smoothies, use frozen fruit.

*Put your ingredients in a blender,
put on the lid, press the button,
and* **whizz!**

Make your own delicious drinks

Blackberry and blueberry

You will need:

60 g (2 oz) blackberries
60 g (2 oz) strawberries
30 g (1 oz) blueberries
¼ banana
4 tbsp blueberry yoghurt
2 tsp honey

Put the berries and banana in a blender with the yoghurt and honey. Blend until all the lumps have gone and it's a lovely deep purple colour.

50

Pineapple, mango, and banana

Banana caramel

You will need:

2½ tbsp dulche de leche
110 ml (4 fl oz) milk
1 large banana
4 tbsp Greek yoghurt

Double strawberry

You will need:

110 g (4 oz) strawberries
¼ banana
6 tbsp strawberry yoghurt
2 tsp honey

You will need:

1 small ripe mango (peeled and stoned)
¼ banana
30 g (1 oz) tinned pineapple chunks
plus 6 tbsp of the pineapple juice
4 tbsp vanilla yoghurt

Put the mango, banana, pineapple plus juice, and yoghurt into a blender and whizz until smooth.

Put 1 tsp of the dulche de leche into a small bowl and mix with 1 tsp of the milk. Set aside while you make the smoothie.

Put the remaining dulche de leche, banana, and yoghurt in a blender and whizz it all together. Add the rest of the milk and whizz again. Drizzle over the thinned dulche de leche before serving.

Put the strawberries, banana, yoghurt, and honey in a blender and blitz until smooth and creamy. If you've got any strawberries left, just dip them in and eat them.

51

Main meals

Here I show you how to make some of my favourite recipes, whether it's healthy fast food like my yummy burgers or fantastic new flavours as in my spicy chicken.
Making your own pasta is fun too. And there's nothing quite as delicious as fresh pasta with my quick-and-easy pesto sauce or hidden-vegetable tomato sauce.
Give Mum and Dad the night off and conjure up some specials in the kitchen…

Sticky chicken drumsticks

You will need:

4 chicken drumsticks
pepper

For the marinade
1 tsp balsamic vinegar
2 tbsp soy sauce
2 tbsp honey
1 small garlic clove
½ tsp grated ginger

To pack this dish with flavour and make it gorgeously sticky, soak the drumsticks in spicy-sweet marinade before cooking. This works the flavours into the meat and adds a lovely glaze.

Cook until golden brown

☆Annabel's Tip
If you are short of bowls, try marinating the chicken in a small plastic food bag.

Making the marinade

Marinating the chicken adds flavour and makes it tender. Sometimes you need to marinade the meat overnight, but this recipe takes only 20 minutes.

root ginger

garlic

soy sauce

balsamic vinegar

honey

Crush

1 First put the balsamic vinegar, soy sauce and honey in a bowl.

2 Remove the papery skin from a clove of garlic and put it in a garlic crusher. Squeeze the garlic into the bowl.

3 Peel a piece of root ginger and grate it on a fine grater. It's easier if you freeze the ginger first. Take care not to scrape your fingers on the blade.

1 Slash the drumsticks with a sharp knife and season with freshly ground black pepper. Put the drumsticks in an ovenproof dish, then pour over the marinade so it coats the chicken. Put the chicken in the fridge for 20 minutes.

2 Preheat the oven to 200°C/400°F/Gas mark 6. Bake the drumsticks in the marinade for 45 minutes or until cooked through, turning and basting every 10 minutes or so.

Pour

55

You will need:

85 g (3 oz) fresh white
breadcrumbs
15 g (½ oz) Parmesan cheese,
grated
1 tbsp chopped parsley
2 skinless chicken breasts
salt and pepper
1 egg, beaten
sunflower oil, for frying

Chicken escalopes

Eat this dish straight from the pan while the coating is still lovely and crisp. Escalopes are made from flattened chicken breasts, so they cook in just a few minutes.

Or try...
... this recipe with pork fillet or medallions instead of chicken. Just give the pork an extra minute or two to cook, and serve with fresh vegetables.

Serve with small new potatoes and fresh green beans

A light coating of breadcrumbs makes it nice and crunchy

1 For the breadcrumbs, whizz together 2 or 3 slices of white bread. Add the Parmesan and parsley.

2 Cover the chicken breasts with clingfilm and bash them with a mallet until they are quite thin.

3 Season the chicken with salt and pepper and dip in the beaten egg.

4 Coat the chicken in the breadcrumb mixture.

Tomato sauce with spaghetti

You will need:

1 tbsp sunflower oil
1 onion, chopped
1 clove garlic, crushed
400 g (14 oz) tin chopped tomatoes
1 tbsp tomato puree
½ tbsp sundried tomato puree
½ tsp sugar
1 tsp fresh thyme
1 tbsp chopped fresh basil
150 g (5½ oz) spaghetti

1 Heat the oil in a pan. Add the onion and garlic and sauté for 2 to 3 minutes. Add the chopped tomatoes and tomato purees, sugar, thyme, and basil. Bring to the boil, cover, and simmer for 20 minutes. Whizz the sauce to a puree.

2 Cook the spaghetti according to the packet instructions. Drain and serve with the sauce.

Perfect with the chicken!

5 Heat the oil in a large frying pan. Fry the chicken on a medium heat for about 3 minutes on each side until golden and cooked through.

These ingredients give a tikka its distinctive flavour

root ginger

ground coriander

garlic

garam masala

mild curry powder

Spicy chicken

This delicious supper is based on an Indian dish called chicken tikka masala. Serve it with basmati rice and poppadoms.

You will need:

2 chicken breasts, cubed
salt and pepper

For the marinade

6 tbsp natural yoghurt
½ tsp grated ginger
1 small clove garlic, crushed
½ tsp mild curry powder

For the sauce

15 g (½ oz) butter
1 medium onion, chopped
1 tsp garam masala
¼ tsp ground coriander
¼ tsp freshly grated ginger
200 ml (7 fl oz) chicken stock
1 tbsp clear honey
1 tbsp tomato puree
1 x 400 g (14 oz) tin tomatoes
150 ml (5½ fl oz) double cream
1 tbsp lemon juice

Marinate

1 For the marinade, mix together the yoghurt, ginger, garlic, and curry powder. Add the chicken and mix to coat. Cover and put in the fridge for 2 hours or overnight.

Sauté

2 To make the sauce, melt the butter and sauté the onion for 5 minutes. Add the garam masala, ground coriander, and ginger and sauté for another 5 minutes.

3 Add the stock, honey, tomato puree, and tinned tomatoes. Stir, then simmer for 15 minutes.

Simmer

4 Add the cream and simmer for 10 more minutes until thick.

5 Line a baking sheet with foil and arrange the marinated chicken cubes on it. Grill for 8 to 10 minutes, turning the pieces over halfway through cooking.

6 Add the cooked chicken and lemon juice to the sauce. Season to taste with salt and pepper. Simmer for a couple of minutes, then serve with fluffy boiled rice.

Spicy tips
Store your spices in airtight jars away from bright sunlight. And don't keep them when they're past their sell-by date, as they've probably lost some of their flavour.

For extra colour...

... add fresh coriander

Sweet and sour pork

This delicious Chinese classic offers an exotic combination of very different flavours – sweet pineapple and sour vinegar.

You will need:

1 egg yolk
1½ tbsp cornflour
pinch of salt
1 tbsp milk
225 g (7½ oz) lean pork, cubed
2 tbsp sunflower oil

For the sauce
1 red onion
½ small red pepper
½ small yellow pepper
1 tbsp sunflower oil
¼ tsp grated ginger
110 ml (4 fl oz) chicken stock
1 tbsp soy sauce
½ tbsp light brown sugar
1 tbsp balsamic vinegar
1 tsp tomato puree
227 g (8 oz) tin pineapple chunks
1 tbsp cornflour mixed with 1 tbsp cold water

1 To make the sauce, first chop the onion roughly. Then chop the red and yellow peppers into squares.

Onion curls
I've decorated this dish with spring onion curls. To make them, cut a spring onion lengthways into thin shreds, soak in iced water, and watch them curl!

stir-fry

2 Heat the oil in a wok or a large frying-pan and stir-fry the onion and peppers for 4 minutes, or until they begin to soften.

3 Add the ginger and cook for 1 minute, then add the stock, soy sauce, sugar, vinegar, tomato puree, and tinned pineapple with its juice.

TRY THIS WITH CHICKEN
This recipe works well with chicken too. Simply swap the pork for 2 sliced chicken breasts.

4 Bring to the boil and simmer for 1 minute, then add the cornflour mixture and simmer a further 2 to 3 minutes, stirring until thickened. Keep the sauce warm over a very low heat while you cook the pork.

5 Whisk the egg yolk, cornflour, salt, and milk together. Add the pork and mix until covered.

Mix the cooked pork with the sauce and serve with spring onion curls

6 Heat the sunflower oil and fry the pork over medium heat for 3 to 4 minutes until it's golden on the outside and cooked right through. You may need to do this in batches so you don't overcrowd the pan.

You will need:

1 medium onion
1 small clove garlic
3 tbsp sunflower oil
1 apple
4 slices bread, crusts removed
4 tbsp grated Parmesan cheese
1 egg yolk
225 g (7½ oz) minced pork
or chicken
1 tsp chopped parsley
2 tsp Worcestershire sauce
1 tbsp tomato puree
1 tbsp honey
¼ tsp grated nutmeg
salt and pepper
flour, for dusting

For the sauce
30 g (1 oz) butter
30 g (1 oz) flour
400 ml (14 fl oz) chicken stock
100 ml (3½ fl oz) double cream
2 tsp soy sauce
1 tsp Worcestershire sauce

Swedish meatballs

For this traditional dish, I like to use pork because it has lots of flavour. But pork can be fatty, so you might like to try chicken instead.

1 Chop the onion finely and crush the garlic. Heat 1 tbsp of the oil and sauté the onion until it's soft. Add the garlic and sauté for another minute. Cool slightly.

2 Peel the apple and grate the flesh (not the core) into a large mixing bowl. Be careful not to grate your fingers too!

3 Tear the bread into small pieces (or use breadcrumbs) and add it to the bowl. Leave the bread and the apple to stand for 5 minutes.

4 Now add the Parmesan, egg yolk, minced pork or chicken, sautéed onion and garlic, parsley, Worcestershire sauce, tomato puree, honey, and nutmeg.

5 Season with a little salt and pepper, then use your hands to mix everything together thoroughly.

6 Scoop up the meat mixture with a teaspoon and roll it into meatballs. Dust them with flour.

7 Heat the remaining oil in a non-stick frying pan and brown the meatballs in batches for 2 to 3 minutes, turning regularly. Drain them on kitchen paper.

8 For the sauce, melt the butter and stir in the flour. Remove from the heat and whisk in the stock, a little at a time. Then add the cream, soy sauce, and Worcestershire sauce. Return to the heat and bring to the boil, stirring constantly. Add the meatballs.

To serve

This meal is rich and filling, so you'll only need small portions. Serve it with green vegetables, such as French beans or broccoli, plus plain boiled rice or noodles.

Cook the dish for 5 to 10 minutes before serving

Lamb tagine

Try my special version of a traditional Moroccan recipe. It's meaty, spicy, and fruity all at once!

You will need:

2 tbsp flour

salt and pepper

450 g (1 lb) diced lamb

2 to 3 tbsp sunflower oil

1 onion, chopped

1 clove garlic, crushed

½ tsp cinnamon

½ tsp cumin

2 tsp mild curry powder

300 ml (10 fl oz) vegetable stock

1 x 400 g (14 oz) tin tomatoes

3 tbsp tomato puree

1 tsp clear honey

½ apple, grated

110 g (4 oz) dried apricots, quartered

☆ Annabel's Tip

This dish freezes well, so make twice the amount you need and freeze some for another day.

1 Mix the flour with ¼ tsp salt and a grinding of black pepper. Toss the lamb in the seasoned flour to coat it.

2 Heat 1 tbsp of the oil and brown the lamb – you may need to do this in batches. Put the browned lamb aside.

Serve with rice or couscous, and garnish with fresh coriander leaves

Stir

3 Heat 1 tbsp oil in a deep pan. Add the onion and cook gently for 8 to 10 minutes until it looks slightly clear. Stir in the garlic, cinnamon, cumin, and curry powder and cook for 2 minutes.

4 Stir in the vegetable stock, a little at a time, then add the tinned tomatoes, tomato puree, honey, and grated apple. Stir everything together.

5 Add the browned lamb to the pan. Bring to the boil, then reduce the heat to low. Cover the pan and cook very gently for 1½ to 2 hours, stirring every 20 minutes.

Simmer

6 Uncover the pan, stir in the apricots, and simmer for a further 30 minutes. Add up to 60 ml (2 fl oz) extra water if the sauce gets too thick. Add salt and pepper to taste.

Best beefburgers

You will need:

1 red onion
1 tbsp olive oil
4 tsp soft light brown sugar
1 tbsp balsamic vinegar
4 sprigs thyme
200 g (7 oz) lean minced beef
40 g (1½ oz) fresh breadcrumbs
1 egg yolk
2 tbsp milk
1 tsp soy sauce
salt and pepper
sunflower oil, for frying

These juicy burgers are made from lean minced beef flavoured with caramelized onion, thyme, and soy sauce. They're delicious fried in a little oil, but if you want to cut down on fat, try grilling them instead.

Chop

1 First peel and chop the onion into small pieces. Heat the oil and gently cook the onion for 8 minutes or until it's soft. Stir in the sugar and balsamic vinegar.

2 Turn up the heat and cook, stirring, for 2 minutes until the onion caramelizes (the sugar on it turns light brown). Stir in the thyme. Then transfer the mixture to a bowl and leave to cool.

3 Add the beef, breadcrumbs, egg yolk, milk, soy sauce, salt and pepper. Mix everything together lightly so the burgers stay soft and moist when they cook.

Flatten

4 Divide the beef mixture into four servings. Roll each one into a ball, then flatten slightly into a burger shape. Cover and chill in the fridge.

5 Oil a frying pan lightly, and cook the burgers over a low heat for 4 to 5 minutes each side. Alternatively, grill the burgers for about 4 minutes on each side.

Put your burger in a bun

Bun top

Sliced onion

Tomato

Burger

Lettuce

Mayonnaise

Bun bottom

Do you like cheese?

For a cheesy surprise, put a small cube of Cheddar into the middle of each burger when you shape it. This will give a melted-cheese centre.

Chicken burger

You will need:

1 tbsp light olive oil
40 g (1½ oz) onion, diced
1 small clove garlic, chopped
225 g (7½ oz) minced chicken or turkey
15 g (½ oz) fresh breadcrumbs
4 fresh sage leaves, chopped
40 g (1½ oz) grated apple
salt and pepper
sunflower oil, for greasing

1 Preheat the oven to 200°C/ 400°F/Gas mark 6. Heat the olive oil in a pan and sauté the onion and garlic for about 2 minutes. Allow to cool.

2 Mix the chicken (or turkey,) breadcrumbs, sage, apple, salt and pepper with the cooled onion and garlic. Shape into 4 burgers.

3 Heat a little oil over a high heat and cook the burgers for 2 minutes each side. Put them on a baking sheet and bake them in the oven for 10 minutes or until completely cooked through. ⚠

Fish parcels with tomato sauce

Wouldn't you love to open a steaming parcel at supper time? Cooking fish in baking paper is a delicious way to seal in its goodness.

You will need:

oil, for greasing
2 skinless, boneless, thick white fish fillets (try cod, haddock, or pollock)
salt and pepper

For the tomato sauce
15 g (½ oz) butter
1 small shallot, finely chopped
4 tomatoes, skinned and chopped
2 tsp tomato puree
2 tbsp fish or vegetable stock
½ tsp lemon juice
pinch of sugar
4 basil leaves, shredded
black olives, sliced

1 Preheat the oven to 200°C/400°F/ Gas mark 6. Grease 2 squares (about 30 cm/12 in) of foil or baking parchment. Sit the fish on the foil and season with salt and pepper.

2 Spoon over the tomato sauce and wrap up like a parcel, folding over the edges to seal them.

Fold up

3 Put the parcel on a baking sheet and bake for 12 to 14 minutes, until the fish is cooked through.

To make the tomato sauce, melt the butter and sauté the shallot for 4 minutes until soft. Add the tomatoes, tomato puree, stock, and lemon juice. Simmer for 3 minutes until thickened. Stir in the sugar, basil, olives, salt and pepper. Leave to cool.

Salmon... in a parcel

This recipe is quick, easy, and healthy – and there are no fishy smells!

1 Preheat the oven to 200°C/400°F/ Gas mark 6. Grease a piece of foil or baking parchment. Put a salmon fillet, salt and pepper, dill, lemon and lime slices on top.

2 Wrap it all up, put it on a baking tray, and cook for 15 minutes.

Lemon

Lime

Dill

From this...

Wrap the fish in a parcel, pop it in the oven – and then just wait!

To this

☆**Annabel's Tip**
Make sure you seal your parcel properly – if there's a hole where steam can escape, your fish may dry out.

Simply unwrap and serve with your favourite vegetables

Fish bites

I've made these moreish mini mouthfuls with cod, but any firm-fleshed fish will work – why not try pollack, haddock, or salmon?

You will need:

300 g (10 oz) skinless fish
2 tbsp plain flour
salt and pepper
2 eggs, beaten
85 g (3 oz) dried breadcrumbs
85 g (3 oz) grated Parmesan cheese
1 tsp paprika
2 or 3 tbsp sunflower oil

Cut the fish into bite-sized pieces.

Cut

2 Put the other ingredients in separate bowls – flour, salt and pepper in one, eggs in another, and breadcrumbs, Parmesan cheese, and paprika in another.

Put flour, salt and pepper in one bowl...

Dip

3 Now dip each piece of fish in the flour, then the egg, then the breadcrumb mix.

...beaten eggs

☆Annabel's Tip

To make a slightly crunchier coating for your bites, dip them in a mixture of half breadcrumbs and half crushed cornflakes.

4 For an extra crispy coating, dip the fish twice in the egg and breadcrumbs.

...and here are breadcrumbs, cheese, and paprika

Dip

go in here...

Dip

5 Heat the oil over medium heat — it's ready if it sizzles when you drop in a few breadcrumbs. Fry the fish bites for 5 minutes, or until they're cooked through, turning them regularly. Drain on kitchen paper before serving.

Delicious crispy, crunchy little nuggets of fish ready in minutes!

☆**Annabel's Tip**
Serve with a simple tartar sauce made with 2 tbsp mayonnaise, 2 chopped gherkins, 1 tsp capers (optional), and 1 tsp snipped chives.

71

Salmon in pastry

These little salmon parcels make perfect picnic food. I've shaped mine into pastry fish, but simple rectangular parcels are lovely too.

You will need:

130 g (4½ oz) baby spinach
15 g (½ oz) butter
1 large shallot or 1 small onion, diced
110 g (4 oz) ricotta cheese
30 g (1 oz) Parmesan cheese, grated
pinch of grated nutmeg
salt and pepper
450 g (1 lb) ready-rolled puff pastry
300 g (10 oz) salmon fillet, divided into 4 equal portions
1 egg, beaten

Sauté

SALMON

You will need skinless, boneless salmon for this dish.

1 First cook the spinach in 1 tbsp water for 2 minutes. Stir and cook for another 2 minutes until wilted. Drain in a colander and leave to cool.

2 Melt the butter and sauté the shallot or onion for 8 to 10 minutes until softened. Transfer to a bowl to cool.

3 Use your hands to squeeze the moisture from the spinach. Then chop it, and add it to the onion along with the ricotta, Parmesan, and nutmeg. Season the mixture with salt and pepper.

4 Divide the pastry into four. Even though it is ready rolled, it still needs to be thinner, so roll each piece to a rectangle about 16 x 40 cm (6 x 16 in). Divide each rolled-out piece into two – these should be about 16 x 20 cm (6 x 8 in).

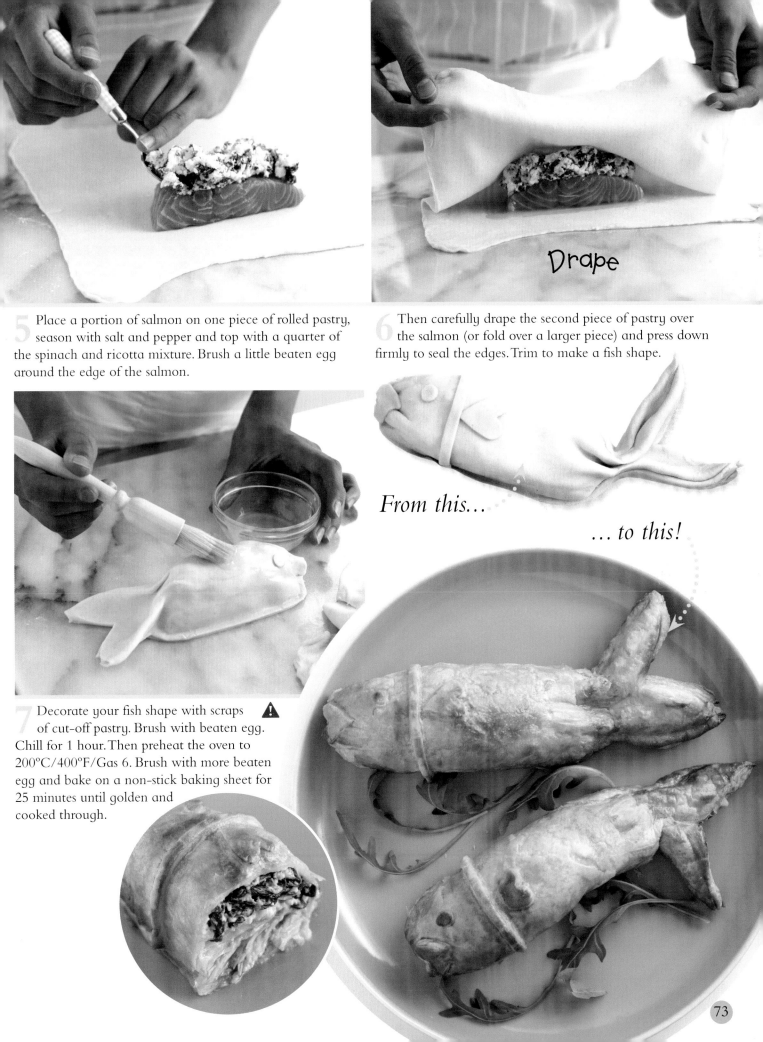

Drape

5 Place a portion of salmon on one piece of rolled pastry, season with salt and pepper and top with a quarter of the spinach and ricotta mixture. Brush a little beaten egg around the edge of the salmon.

6 Then carefully drape the second piece of pastry over the salmon (or fold over a larger piece) and press down firmly to seal the edges. Trim to make a fish shape.

From this...

... to this!

7 Decorate your fish shape with scraps of cut-off pastry. Brush with beaten egg. Chill for 1 hour. Then preheat the oven to 200°C/400°F/Gas 6. Brush with more beaten egg and bake on a non-stick baking sheet for 25 minutes until golden and cooked through.

Pizza Margherita

Plain cheese-and-tomato (Margherita) pizza is hard to beat. It's totally yummy just as it is, but you might want to experiment with a few of your own toppings...

You will need:

bread dough (page 42)
oil, for greasing
tomato sauce (page 82)
225 g (7½ oz)
mozzarella cheese, sliced
16 cherry tomatoes

1 For the dough, use my bread recipe on page 42, but replace the butter with 2 tbsp oil. After the first prove, knock back and divide into 4 pieces for large pizzas, or 8 for small ones.

2 Preheat oven to 220°C/425°F/Gas mark 7. Oil a couple of large baking sheets. Roll out the dough into circles, then place them on the baking sheets.

3 Spread a thin layer of tomato sauce on each pizza. Top with mozzarella cheese and halved cherry tomatoes. (Or try a mix of cheeses such as mozzarella with grated Cheddar or Parmesan.) Bake in the oven for 10 to 12 minutes.

Scatter fresh basil leaves over your baked pizza

☆Annabel's Tip

Make tomato sauce and store it in the freezer until you need it. Alternatively, use passata sauce from the supermarket.

Season with *freshly ground black pepper*

Homemade pasta

For this recipe I've used "00" flour, but if you can't find it use bread flour – the pasta won't be as smooth but will still taste good.

200 g (7 oz) "00" flour
plus extra for dusting

2 eggs

½ tsp salt

2 tsp olive oil

> ### Made by hand
> *You can make the pasta by hand or in a food processor. And it can be rolled out by hand or using a pasta machine.*

Well

Stir

1 Whisk together the eggs and oil. Put the flour on a work surface and make a well in the centre. Carefully pour the egg mixture into the well.

2 Gently stir the flour into the egg, bringing in a little flour at a time.

Keep mixing to make a smooth dough

3 Gradually work more flour into the egg mixture. Keep going until all the flour is combined.

Mix

Kneaded dough

4 If you want to, mix the eggs and flour using your fingers. Roll the dough into a ball.

5 Put the dough on a clean surface and knead for 5 minutes or until it feels smooth and silky.

6 Wrap the kneaded dough in clingfilm and put in the fridge to rest for 30 minutes.

1 Cut the dough into four. Roll one piece at a time, keeping the rest of the dough wrapped in clingfilm.

2 Roll the dough into a rough rectangle approximately 6 x 10 cm (2½ x 4 in).

3 Set the rollers of a pasta machine on the widest setting and roll the dough through.

4 Fold the dough into a rectangle and roll again. Reduce the rollers by one notch and roll through again. Keep reducing the width of the rollers until you reach the right thickness.

5 It is best to roll the dough twice through each width (apart from the narrowest one). If the pasta gets too long to handle, cut it in half crossways.

No pasta machine?
You can also roll out the dough by hand using a rolling pin. Be careful not to tear the dough as it gets thinner and thinner.

Roll slowly

✰ Annabel's Tip
For your first try, you'll need someone to help you feed dough into the machine, turn the handle, and support the papery dough that comes out.

Making tagliatelle

1 Roll the dough through the narrowest setting. Dust it with flour.

2 Fold the dough loosely and cut it into narrow strips.

3 Open out the strips by shaking the pasta gently.

The pasta needs to dry slightly before cooking

Hang it to dry for 15 to 30 minutes

The pasta should feel dry to the touch

You can hang it on a wooden spoon suspended between two candlesticks!

To cook

Bring a large pan of salted water to the boil. Add the pasta and boil for 2 minutes. Drain and toss with one of the pasta sauces over the page.

Pesto sauce

Adding parsley helps to give pesto its lovely green colour. There is enough pesto here for four servings.

Whizz ingredients together

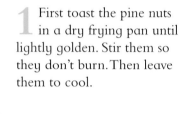

1 First toast the pine nuts in a dry frying pan until lightly golden. Stir them so they don't burn. Then leave them to cool.

2 Put the Parmesan, garlic, parsley, basil, sugar, and cooled pine nuts into a food processor and whizz until finely chopped. Slowly add the olive oil while the motor is whizzing. Add the water, salt and pepper.

Now use your fresh pesto on a bowl of pasta

3 Cook pasta according to the packet instructions. Drain and put back into the pan. Add the pesto and toss together. Sprinkle with extra Parmesan to serve.

Tomato and vegetable sauce

You will need:

1 tbsp olive oil
1 red onion, chopped
1 carrot, peeled and grated
½ small leek, thinly sliced
¼ red pepper, diced
1 clove garlic, crushed
1 tbsp balsamic vinegar
1 tbsp soft light brown sugar
400 g (14 oz) tin chopped tomatoes
2 tbsp tomato puree
150 ml (5½ fl oz) vegetable stock
salt and pepper

1 Heat the oil in a large pan and sauté the onion, carrot, leek, and pepper for 10 minutes until soft. Add the garlic and cook for one minute, then add the vinegar and sugar and cook for 2 minutes until the vinegar has evaporated. ⚠

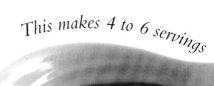

This makes 4 to 6 servings

2 Stir in the tomatoes, tomato puree, and vegetable stock. Simmer for 25 to 30 minutes until the sauce has thickened. Season with salt and pepper. The sauce can be used as is or pureed for a smoother texture.

Cheese sauce

Serves 4 to 6

You will need:

40 g (1½ oz) butter
40 g (1½ oz) flour
500 ml (17 fl oz) milk
60 g (2 oz) Cheddar, grated
30 g (1 oz) Parmesan, grated
60 g (2 oz) Gruyère, grated
½ tsp Dijon mustard
4 tbsp double cream
¼ tsp nutmeg
salt and white pepper

1 Melt the butter and stir in the flour. Turn off the heat and whisk in the milk, a little at a time, to make a smooth sauce. Then cook over a medium heat, stirring constantly until the sauce thickens and bubbles.

2 Then stir in the Cheddar, Parmesan, and Gruyère cheeses, mustard, cream, and nutmeg. Season with salt and pepper (white pepper is nice as it doesn't show in the sauce).

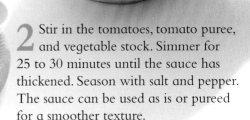

You will need:

For the roasted vegetables

2 medium courgettes, sliced
2 red peppers, cut into squares
1 large red onion, cut into chunks
2 tbsp olive oil
salt and pepper

For the tomato sauce

1 tbsp olive oil
1 large onion, chopped
½ leek, thinly sliced
1 medium carrot, grated
1 celery stalk, thinly sliced
1 clove garlic, crushed
2 x 400 g (14 oz) tins chopped tomatoes
2 tsp balsamic vinegar
1 tbsp sugar
2 tbsp tomato puree
2 tbsp sundried tomato puree
salt and pepper

For the cheese sauce

40 g (1½ oz) butter
40 g (1½ oz) plain flour
600 ml (1 pt) milk
60 g (2 oz) Cheddar cheese, grated
60 g (2 oz) Gruyère cheese, grated
pinch nutmeg
¼ tsp Dijon mustard
85 g (3 oz) mascarpone cheese or crème fraiche
30 g (1 oz) Parmesan cheese, grated
salt and pepper

To put it together

olive oil, for greasing
8 to 9 sheets lasagne
40 g (1½ oz) Parmesan cheese, grated

☆Annabel's Tip

When you make this lasagne, cut your vegetables to roughly the same thickness so they all cook through properly.

Vegetable lasagne

This dish is packed with vegetables – chunky roasted ones you can see, and finely blended ones in the sauce. Serve it with crusty bread.

1   Preheat the oven to 200°C/400°F/ Gas mark 6. To roast the vegetables, put the courgettes, peppers, onion, olive oil, salt and pepper in a roasting pan. Gently mix everything together.

2   Cover with foil and roast for 30 minutes. Uncover and roast for a further 20 minutes until the vegetables are soft and browning at the edges. Remove from the oven and cool slightly.

3   To make the tomato sauce, heat the oil and sauté the onion, leek, carrot, and celery until soft. Add the garlic and cook for one minute.

4   Now add the tinned tomatoes, vinegar, sugar, tomato puree, sundried tomato puree, salt and pepper. Simmer for 30 minutes until thick.

5 Leave the mixture to cool slightly, then blend to a puree using a hand blender or a liquidizer.

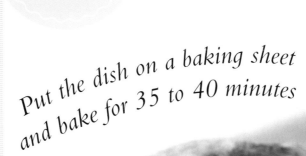

6 For the cheese sauce, melt the butter and stir in the flour. Remove from the heat and whisk in the milk, a little at a time, to avoid lumps.

7 Put the pan over a medium heat and cook, stirring, until the sauce thickens. Take off the heat and stir in the Cheddar and Gruyère so they melt. Then stir in the nutmeg, mustard, mascarpone, and most of the Parmesan. Season with salt and pepper.

PUTTING IT ALL TOGETHER

Oil a baking dish. Put a third of the cheese sauce in the bottom. Then add:

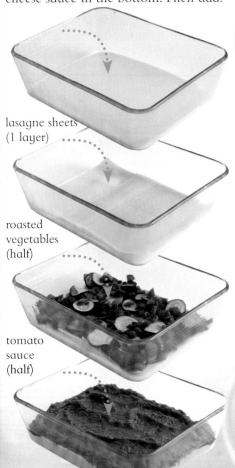

lasagne sheets (1 layer)

roasted vegetables (half)

tomato sauce (half)

Repeat this layering, finishing with the cheese sauce. Then sprinkle the rest of the grated Parmesan over the top.

You need an oblong dish about 24 x 19 cm (9½ x 7½ in) and 7 cm (3 in) deep.

Put the dish on a baking sheet and bake for 35 to 40 minutes

83

Risotto primavera

This Italian classic is a super-tasty, meat-free, meal-in-a-bowl. It's made with meltingly soft rice, summer vegetables, and Parmesan cheese.

You will need:

1 small carrot
1 small leek
1 small onion
1 small garlic clove
½ medium courgette
15 g (½ oz) butter

1 tbsp olive oil
225 g (7½ oz) risotto rice
1.1 litre (2 pt) hot vegetable stock
85 g (3 oz) frozen peas
60 g (2 oz) grated Parmesan cheese, plus extra to serve
freshly ground black pepper

Scatter cheese shavings on top before serving

☆**Annabel's Tip**
For perfect risotto, the rice should be al dente. This means soft but not mushy – when you bite in, it should still be a little firm.

Slice

1 Dice the carrot, then thinly slice the leek and the onion, crush the garlic, and dice the courgette.

2 Melt the butter in a large saucepan. Add the oil, then sauté the onion for 4 to 5 minutes until it's soft and translucent. Add the leek, carrot, and garlic and sauté for another 2 to 3 minutes until the leek has softened.

3 Stir in the rice and cook for 1 minute, then stir in a ladleful of stock and cook slowly until the liquid is absorbed, stirring all the time.

4 Add the rest of the stock a ladleful at a time – wait until it is absorbed before adding more. Stir the rice regularly during cooking. After about 18 minutes it will be almost cooked through.

5 Add the diced courgette and peas plus more stock if necessary. Cook for a further 4 minutes or until the vegetables are cooked through. Remove from the heat and stir in the cheese. Season with pepper, then serve.

Veggie fajitas

I've filled my Mexican-style tortillas with colourful vegetables in a mildly spicy sauce. These are a bit messy to eat – but they're worth it!

You will need:

4 tortilla wraps
60 g (2 oz) Cheddar cheese, grated

For the salsa

2 tomatoes, diced
2 spring onions, finely sliced
2 tsp lemon juice
1 tsp olive oil
¼ red chilli, deseeded and diced
1 tbsp chopped coriander

For the filling

1 medium red onion
½ red pepper
½ yellow pepper
½ orange pepper
1 tbsp sunflower oil
⅛ tsp cumin
pinch of paprika
1 tbsp balsamic vinegar
2 tsp soft light brown sugar
salt and pepper

1 To make the salsa, simply mix the ingredients together in a bowl.

2 For the filling, thinly slice the onion. Deseed and thinly slice the peppers.

3 Heat the oil in a wok or large frying pan and stir-fry the onion and peppers for about 4 minutes until soft. Add the cumin and paprika and cook for 1 minute, then stir in the balsamic vinegar and boil until evaporated. Stir in the sugar and season with salt and pepper.

4 Warm the wraps in a microwave or dry frying pan, then divide the fillings between them.

☆Annabel's Tip
Try adding sliced avocado to your fajita. Avocados are packed with essential vitamins and minerals.

Serve with soured cream

Start with the onion and pepper mixture...

...then spoon over the salsa.

Next, scatter over grated cheese...

...and finally roll up your wrap!

Sweet treats

Learn how to make delicious treats for the whole family to enjoy. Follow my simple instructions and you'll be able to make perfect muffins, cakes, cookies, and fruit tarts. Why not organize a cookie and cake exchange where everyone brings their own favourite recipe and ingredients and you all learn how to make the recipes and share out the treats to take home? Baking has never been so easy or so much fun...

Best muffins ever

Here are five kinds of yummy muffin – the step-by-step pictures show how to make plain ones, and fancy ones are on the facing page.

You will need:

150 g (5½ oz) plain flour
1 tsp baking powder
⅛ tsp bicarbonate of soda
¼ tsp salt
85 g (3 oz) caster sugar
85 g (3 oz) butter, melted and cooled slightly
1 egg
4 tbsp milk
1 tsp vanilla extract
3 tbsp natural yoghurt

1 Preheat the oven to 180°C/350°F/ Gas mark 4. Line a muffin tin with paper muffin cases.

2 Put the flour, baking powder, bicarbonate of soda, salt, and sugar in a large bowl. Mix them together.

3 In another bowl, put the butter, egg, milk, vanilla, and yoghurt, and whisk them together.

4 Pour the whisked butter mixture onto the flour mixture.

5 Stir everything together. Be careful not to over mix – there should still be a few lumps.

SPICY APPLE AND RAISIN
Add 1½ tsp mixed spice, 60 g (2 oz) raisins, and ½ peeled, chopped apple to the flour.

ORANGE AND CRANBERRY
Add 60 g (2 oz) dried cranberries and the zest of 1 orange to the flour. Replace the milk with 4 tbsp orange juice.

DOUBLE CHOCOLATE
Replace 30 g (1 oz) flour with 30 g (1 oz) cocoa powder. Replace the caster sugar with soft light brown sugar. Add 85 g (3 oz) chopped milk chocolate to the flour. Increase the milk to 5 tbsp.

6 Spoon the mixture into the muffin cases. Bake for 18 to 20 minutes until risen and firm to the touch. Cool for 5 minutes in the tin, then remove and put on a wire rack to cool completely.

☆ **Don't forget...**
... to add the extra ingredients for these flavoured muffins at step 2 in the instructions.

Spicy apple and raisin

Orange and cranberry

Lemon and blueberry

Double chocolate

LEMON AND BLUEBERRY
Add 85 g (3 oz) blueberries and the grated zest of 1 lemon to the flour. Top each muffin with ¼ tsp demerara sugar before baking.

My favourite carrot cake...

You will need:

For the cake

300 g (10 oz) peeled carrots (about 3 large carrots)

200 g (7 oz) caster sugar (golden caster works well)

200 g (7 oz) plain flour

¼ tsp salt

2 tsp baking powder

¼ tsp bicarbonate of soda

2 tsp mixed spice (or 1 tsp ground ginger and 1 tsp cinnamon)

85 g (3 oz) raisins

100 ml (3½ fl oz) sunflower oil, plus extra for greasing

3 medium eggs

1 tsp vanilla extract

For the icing

60 g (2 oz) butter, softened

225 g (7½ oz) mascarpone or cream cheese

110 g (4 oz) icing sugar

3 to 4 drops vanilla extract

... and it really *is* my favourite because of its subtle spicy flavour. The carrots in this recipe are what make it scrumptiously moist and sweet.

1 Preheat the oven to 180°C/350°F/ Gas mark 4. Grease a 20 cm (8 in) round cake tin and line the base with baking parchment. Grate the carrots.

2 Put the grated carrot in a bowl. Add the sugar, flour, salt, baking powder, bicarbonate of soda, and mixed spice.

Mix

3 Then add the raisins and mix everything together...

Pour

When the cake is cool...

...spread the icing over the top using a spatula

... as you mix, the juice from the carrots makes the mixture moist and gooey!

4 Whisk together the oil, eggs, and vanilla in a jug, then pour onto the carrot mixture and stir. Pour into the prepared tin and bake for 40 minutes.

5 To make the icing In a large bowl, mix together the butter and cheese using a wooden spoon. Add the icing sugar and vanilla and stir until smooth.

☆**Annabel's Tip**
When your cake is cooked, it should be risen and firm to the touch. Push a skewer into the centre – if it comes out clean, the cake is ready.

Decorate with carrots made from fondant icing tinted with food colouring

You will need:

200 g (7 oz) unsalted butter, plus extra for greasing
75 g (2½ oz) plain chocolate
250 g (8 oz) caster sugar
4 eggs, lightly beaten
200 g (7 oz) self-raising flour
large pinch of salt
2 tbsp soured cream
1 tsp vanilla extract
1½ tbsp cocoa powder

For the chocolate icing

85 g (3 oz) plain chocolate
3 tbsp milk
2 tbsp golden syrup

Marble cake

Inside this cake are swirls of chocolate and vanilla. These are made from the same basic mixture, but have different flavourings.

1 Preheat the oven to 180°C/350°F/Gas 4. Lightly grease a Bundt tin 21½ cm (8½ in) across and 10 cm (4 in) high.

☆**Annabel's Tip**
You can mix this cake using a wooden spoon. But you might need some help as it will make your arm ache!

2 Melt the chocolate in a bowl set over a pan of warm water. Then set it aside to cool.

3 Cream the butter and sugar until light and fluffy.

94

4 Beat in the eggs, a little at a time. If the mixture curdles (separates) add a spoonful of flour and carry on beating.

5 Then sift over the flour and salt. Fold this in, then add the soured cream and fold this in too.

6 Divide the mixture equally between two bowls. Stir the vanilla into one of the bowls of mixture.

7 Add the cocoa powder and chocolate to the other bowl. Stir to combine.

Now spoon your mixtures into the prepared cake tin...

8 Put alternating spoonfuls of chocolate and vanilla in the tin. You can do this in two layers, if you like.

9 Use a skewer or wooden spoon to swirl the mixtures into each other for a marble effect. Bake for 50 to 55 minutes or until the cake is risen and firm to the touch.

To decorate...

... sift over a little icing sugar...

Is it cooked? Push in a skewer. If it comes out clean, it's cooked.

How to make chocolate icing

For the icing put the chocolate, milk, and golden syrup into a heatproof bowl set over a pan of simmering water. Leave to melt, stirring occasionally. Then cool the icing slightly and drizzle it over the cake.

Alternatively, melt 60 g (2 oz) milk chocolate in a bowl set over a pan of hot water. Leave to cool slightly. Beat 85 g (3 oz) softened butter until pale and fluffy. Then beat in 75 g (2½ oz) icing sugar, a little at a time. Stir in the cooled chocolate and spread over the cake.

10 Cool in the tin for 20 minutes. Then turn out onto a cooling rack and leave to cool completely before icing.

☆**Annabel's Tip**
This cake freezes well. Thaw it out, then ice it just before serving.

... or drizzle with chocolate icing

You will need:

- 110 g (4 oz) butter, softened
- 110 g (4 oz) caster sugar
- 110 g (4 oz) plain flour
- 2 tsp baking powder
- ¼ tsp salt
- 2 medium eggs (at room temperature)
- 1 tsp vanilla extract

Vanilla cupcakes

This is a basic cupcake recipe. You can change the ingredients slightly to make different-flavoured cakes, or add all sorts of icings and decorations so every cake is a mini masterpiece!

Vanilla cupcakes

1 Preheat the oven to 180°C/350°F/ Gas 4. Line a tin with paper cases.

2 Put the butter and sugar in a bowl and beat until pale and fluffy.

Sift

3 Sift the flour, baking powder, and salt onto the butter mixture.

4 Add the eggs and vanilla and beat until just combined.

5 Spoon the mixture into the paper cases. Bake for 18 to 20 minutes until risen, golden, and firm to the touch.

For chocolate cakes...

... replace 30 g (1 oz) of the flour with cocoa.

Add a filling

Cut a cone from the middle of each cake. Fill the hole with jam, lemon curd, or icing, and replace the plug. Ice the top with buttercream.

A filled cupcake

Buttercream icing

For plain buttercream, beat 110 g (4 oz) butter until soft, then beat in 110 g (4 oz) icing sugar, a tablespoon at a time.

For vanilla buttercream, add ½ tsp vanilla and beat to combine.

For lemon buttercream, beat in 1 tbsp lemon juice – add 1 tsp at a time and taste after each addition.

For chocolate buttercream, beat in ¼ tsp vanilla, 60 g (2 oz) melted and cooled milk chocolate, and 2 tbsp cocoa powder.

Cool cakes on a wire rack before decorating

For lemon cakes...
... reduce vanilla to ½ tsp and add the finely grated zest of 1 large lemon with the eggs.

Fondant icing

You can buy ready-made fondant icing at the supermarket. If you want to add colour, knead in a few drops of food colouring. Then roll it out and use it to decorate your cupcakes.

Butterfly cake

You'll need about 250 g (8 oz) fondant icing for this. Cut out a set of wings for each cake. Use sweets to make each butterfly's body, and draw on wing decorations with writing icing.

Chocolate sweets

Chocolate monkey

For this, you'll need about 110 g (4 oz) yellow fondant icing. Cut out a yellow circle for each monkey. Cover chocolate cupcakes with chocolate buttercream. Stick on a fondant-icing muzzle, chocolate-button ears, chocolate-chip eyes, nose, and hair, and draw on a mouth with icing.

Chocolate chips

Giant chocolate buttons

Cupcake icing ideas

These cakes are made using my basic cupcake recipe. It's the icing that makes them special. Swirl it on using a piping bag and nozzle – but practise on a plate first!

Chocolate curls
To make curls of chocolate you need a bar of chocolate and a potato peeler. Then all you do is run the peeler down the back of the chocolate bar. Shake your curls onto a plate and refrigerate until needed.

Top it off with fruit

Chocolate curls

Vanilla

Decorate with sprinkles

For perfect piping, first choose a nozzle – large ones for thick swirls, and small ones for delicate little blobs and stars. Put the nozzle in the piping bag, then half fill the bag with icing. Squeeze the bag from the top as you pipe.

☆ **Annabel's Tip**
You can make any colour icing simply by mixing in a few drops of food colouring. Add a few sprinkles to really add sparkle to your cakes.

Chocolate cream

Lovely lemon

Caramel

Colour your icing

Raspberry and chocolate

Fillings and flavours

Raspberry and chocolate cupcakes
Use vanilla cupcakes. Fill each one with 1 tsp raspberry jam and ice with chocolate buttercream.

Lemon cupcakes
Use lemon cupcakes. Fill with 1 tsp lemon curd and ice with lemon buttercream.

Caramel cupcakes
Use vanilla cupcakes. Fill with 1 tsp dulche de leche and ice with vanilla buttercream. Top with sliced banana.

Chocolate-cream cupcakes
Use chocolate cupcakes. Mix 85 g (3 oz) mascarpone cheese with 2 tbsp cream and ¼ tsp vanilla. Put in the centre of each cupcake. Ice with chocolate buttercream.

Chocolate orange brownies

You will need:

225 g (7½ oz) butter
200 g (7 oz) dark chocolate
275 g (9 oz) soft light brown sugar
zest of 1 large orange
juice of ½ orange
4 eggs
1 tsp pure vanilla extract
large pinch of salt
110 g (4 oz) plain flour
30 g (1 oz) cocoa powder
1 tsp baking powder
110 g (4 oz) white chocolate chips
or chopped white chocolate

Fudgy or cakey?

For a fudgy brownie, cook for 30 minutes. (When you push a skewer into the mixture, soft batter will stick to it.) For a more cakey brownie, cook for 35 minutes. (Soft crumbs will stick to the skewer.)

For a special treat, bake a batch of rich brownies. Decide whether you like them fudgy or cakey, and adjust the cooking time to suit.

1 Preheat the oven to 180°C/350°F/ Gas mark 4. Line a 20 cm (8 in) square cake tin with baking parchment, making sure the parchment comes up the sides of the tin.

2 Put the butter, dark chocolate, and sugar in a large heatproof bowl and set it over (but not in) a saucepan of warm water.

Melt

3 Let the butter and chocolate melt, stirring occasionally. Remove bowl from saucepan and leave to cool.

4 Prepare the orange zest and juice. Then whisk these together with the eggs, vanilla, and salt until combined.

5 Whisk the egg mixture into the cooled melted chocolate.

Sift

6 Sift the flour, cocoa, and baking powder onto the chocolate mixture and fold it in.

7 Now add the white chocolate chips and fold these in too.

8 Pour into the prepared tin and bake for 30 to 35 minutes. Let the brownies cool completely in the tin.

To serve, tip the cool brownies out of the tin and cut into squares

Triple chocolate chip cookies

When they're all warm and soft, these cookies are irresistible. They freeze well – if there are any left!

You will need:

110 g (4 oz) butter, softened
110 g (4 oz) caster sugar
110 g (4 oz) soft light brown sugar
1 egg
1 tsp vanilla
150 g (5½ oz) plain flour
60 g (2 oz) rolled oats
½ tsp baking powder
¼ tsp salt
30 g (1 oz) milk chocolate chips
30 g (1 oz) dark chocolate chips
30 g (1 oz) white chocolate chips

1 Cream together the butter and sugars until pale and fluffy.

2 Mix together the egg and vanilla and beat into the butter mixture.

3 Add the flour, oats, baking powder, and salt and fold in gently.

4 Then add the chocolate chips and fold them in too.

5 Line baking sheets with parchment. Arrange heaped tablespoons of the mixture about 5 cm (2 in) apart, as the cookies spread during cooking.

ORANGE AND CHOCOLATE
Replace the milk and white chocolate chips with 85 g (3 oz) milk-chocolate chips and the grated zest of 1 orange.

CHOCOLATE AND CRANBERRIES
Replace the milk and dark chocolate chips with 30 g (1 oz) white chocolate chips and 60 g (2 oz) dried cranberries.

CHOCOLATE AND RAISINS
Replace the dark and white chocolate chips with 30 g (1 oz) milk chocolate chips and 60 g (2 oz) raisins.

Leave space to spread out

Now chill

6 Chill the cookies in the freezer for 10 to 15 minutes, or in the fridge for 30 minutes. Preheat the oven to 180°C/350°F/Gas mark 4.

7 Bake for 12 minutes until golden around the edges. Leave to cool slightly on the baking sheets, then transfer to wire racks to cool completely.

Ginger biscuits

These crispy, spicy biscuits are easy to cut into exciting novelty shapes, but they're just as nice in plain rounds, squares, or fingers.

You will need:

400 g (14 oz) plain flour
¾ tsp bicarbonate of soda
1 tsp cinnamon
2 tsp ground ginger
½ tsp mixed spice
½ tsp salt
170 g (6 oz) unsalted butter, at room temperature
110 g (4 oz) soft dark brown sugar
1 egg
110 g (4 oz) black treacle

1 Sift the flour, bicarbonate of soda, cinnamon, ginger, mixed spice, and salt into a bowl and set aside.

2 In another bowl, beat together the butter and sugar until they are light and fluffy.

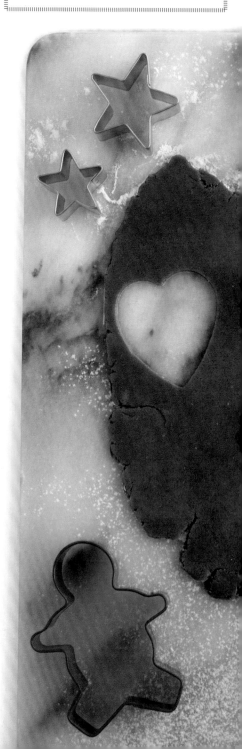

3 Add the egg and treacle to the butter mix. Beat thoroughly. (Before you measure the treacle, dip your spoon into oil so it doesn't stick.)

4 Gradually add the flour mixture – just a few tablespoons at a time at first and then in larger batches. Mix thoroughly.

5 Once the dough is well mixed and smooth, flatten it into 2 round shapes about 2½ cm (1 in) thick, and wrap them in clingfilm. Put them in the fridge for at least an hour to firm up.

6 Preheat the oven to 170°C/325°F/Gas mark 3. Dust a work surface lightly with flour, then roll out each round of dough to a thickness of about 3 mm (⅛ in). Cut out shapes using plain or novelty biscuit cutters.

7 Line baking sheets with baking paper, and arrange the biscuits on top. Bake for 12 to 15 minutes. Leave the biscuits to cool slightly on the trays before turning onto racks to cool completely. Try icing with royal icing or writing icing.

Tropical cereal bars

You will need:

85 g (3 oz) butter
85 g (3 oz) brown sugar
3 tbsp maple syrup
½ tsp salt
30 g (1 oz) dried mango
40 g (1½ oz) dried apricot
110 g (4 oz) oats
30 g (1 oz) Rice Krispies
30 g (1 oz) desiccated coconut
30 g (1 oz) sultanas

Tuck these sweet, crunchy, high-fibre snacks into your lunch box, or grab one whenever you need an energy boost. There are two recipes here – both can be stored for up to a week in the fridge.

☆**Annabel's Tip**

Any porridge oats will work in this recipe, but I like the big whole oat flakes best, as they give the bars a coarse, chewy texture.

Cool completely in the tin, then lift out and cut into bars

Apricot

Sultana

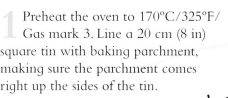

1 Preheat the oven to 170°C/325°F/Gas mark 3. Line a 20 cm (8 in) square tin with baking parchment, making sure the parchment comes right up the sides of the tin.

Mmmm – sweet and sticky

2 Put the butter, sugar, maple syrup, and salt in a saucepan. Heat gently, stirring occasionally, until it's all melted. Then leave it to cool slightly.

3 Chop the dried mango and apricot into small pieces. Put these in a bowl along with the oats, Rice Krispies, desiccated coconut, and sultanas. Pour on the melted butter mixture.

4 Stir well so the butter and sugar are combined thoroughly with the dry ingredients.

5 Spoon the mixture into the prepared tin and press down well (a potato masher is good for this). Bake for 25-30 minutes until it's golden around the edges.

CRANBERRY BAR

85 g (3 oz) butter
85 g (3 oz) brown sugar
3 tbsp maple syrup
½ tsp salt
130 g (4½ oz) oats
30 g (1 oz) chopped dried apricots
30 g (1 oz) raisins
30 g (1 oz) dried cranberries
30 g (1 oz) desiccated coconut
30 g (1 oz) pumpkin seeds

Put the butter, sugar, and syrup in a large saucepan and heat gently until melted. Remove from the heat and stir in the other ingredients. Then cook as tropical cereal bars above.

You will need:

For the pastry
170 g (6 oz) plain flour, plus extra for dusting
1 tbsp caster sugar
large pinch salt
110 g (4 oz) cold butter, cut into 1 cm (½ in) cubes
1 egg yolk, whisked together with 1 tbsp cold water

For the apple filling
900 g (2 lbs) cooking apples
110 g (4 oz) sugar
½ tsp cinnamon
15 g (½ oz) butter
1 egg, beaten with 1 tbsp water

Homemade apple pie

This traditional family dessert is a big favourite in North America – and at my house! I've used cooking apples here, but eating apples work well too – just add a little less sugar.

Make the filling

1 For the filling, first peel and core the apples.

Slice

2 Slice the apples into pieces. (Stop them turning brown by putting them in a bowl of water mixed with 1 tbsp lemon juice.)

Make the pastry

1 Stir together the flour, sugar, and salt in a large bowl. Add the cubes of butter and rub in until the mixture looks like fine breadcrumbs.

2 Stir in the egg mixture to make a soft dough. Add extra water, a teaspoon at a time, if necessary. Bring the dough together with your hands. Form into a disk about 1 cm (½ in) thick. Wrap in clingfilm and chill for 30 minutes.

3 Mix together the sugar and cinnamon. (If you are soaking the apples, drain and pat them dry.)

4 Put half the sliced apples in the bottom of a pie dish that's about 25 x 18 x 7 cm (10 x 7 x 3 in).

5 Sprinkle over half the sugar. Add the rest of the apples, then the remaining sugar. Dot with butter.

6 Flour a board and rolling pin. Roll out the pastry until it is slightly larger than the dish.

7 Brush the lip of the dish with beaten egg. Lift the pastry on the rolling pin and lay it over the filling.

8 Cover the filling completely.

9 Cut away excess pastry with a knife.

10 Crimp the edge of the pastry to seal it to the dish.

Decorate

Cook on a hot baking sheet for 20 minutes at 200°C/400°F/ Gas 6. Reduce heat to 180°C/350°F/Gas 4 and bake for another 40 minutes.

Delicious served with custard!

11 Decorate with pastry scraps, brush with egg, and cut a steam hole.

111

Little fruit tarts

These little tarts are made with sweet shortcrust pastry...

Shape

1 To make the pastry, stir together the flour and salt, then rub in the butter until the mixture looks like fine breadcrumbs. Stir in the icing sugar.

2 Whisk together the egg yolk, water, and vanilla. Add 2 tbsp to the bowl and mix with a knife. The pastry should stick together, if not, add more egg mixture a tsp at a time. Form into a ball.

3 Divide the pastry into 8 roughly equal pieces and shape into flat balls. Wrap each piece in clingfilm. Chill in the fridge for 30 minutes.

7 Take the cases out of the oven ⚠ and leave to cool in the tins for 20 minutes. Then remove from the tins and transfer to a wire rack.

8 For the filling, whisk together the mascarpone, cream or crème fraiche, sugar, and vanilla until slightly thickened.

9 Spoon the filling into the pastry cases until they are about half full. Top with different types of fresh fruit.

Leave the pastry cases until cold

Spread a little creamy filling in the base

Top with your favourite fruit...

kiwi fruit and green grapes

You will need:

For the pastry
170 g (6 oz) plain flour, plus extra for dusting

large pinch of salt
110 g (4 oz) cold unsalted butter
3 tbsp icing sugar

1 egg yolk
1 tbsp cold water
2 to 3 drops vanilla extract

... and filled with jewel-coloured fruits.

Roll

4 Lightly dust a surface and your rolling pin with flour. Then roll out each piece of chilled pastry to around 3 mm (⅛ in) thick. It should be just a little bigger than the tin.

5 Use the pastry to line 9 cm (3½ in) tart tins. Don't worry if you make a hole – simply squash a bit of spare pastry over the gap. Preheat the oven to 180°C/350°F/Gas mark 4.

6 Trim off the excess pastry. Chill the cases for 10 minutes, then prick the bottoms of the cases with a fork. Put on a baking sheet and bake for 15 to 18 minutes until golden brown.

For the filling
100 g (3½ oz) mascarpone cheese
100 ml (3½ fl oz) double cream or
100 g (3½ oz) crème fraiche

1 tbsp icing sugar
2 to 3 drops vanilla extract
250 g (8 oz) fresh fruit

Dust with icing sugar just before serving

raspberries, strawberries, and redcurrants

papaya and mango

blueberries and blackberries

113

You will need:

3 egg whites
pinch of salt
170 g (6 oz) caster sugar
½ tsp cornflour
½ tsp lemon juice
150 ml (5½ fl oz) double cream
150 g (5½ oz) mixed berries

Mini meringues

This recipe comes from Australia where it's called pavlova, after a Russian ballet dancer. Make four small meringues or one big one.

1 Cover a baking sheet with parchment. Draw 4 guide circles, each about 7 cm (3 in) across. Turn the parchment over – you should still be able to see the circles.

2 To separate the eggs, tip each yolk from one half shell to the other, letting the white fall into a bowl. You only need the whites for this recipe.

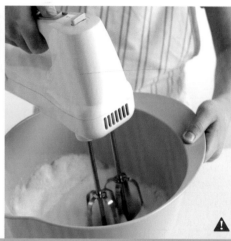

3 Preheat the oven to 140°C/275°F/ Gas mark 1. Add a pinch of salt to the egg whites and whisk to stiff peaks. Whisk in 2 tbsp sugar and whisk back to stiff peaks, then whisk in another 2 tbsp sugar and whisk to stiff peaks again.

4 Fold in the remaining sugar, then sift over the cornflour and fold that in too, along with the lemon juice.

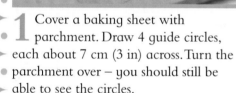

Fold gently

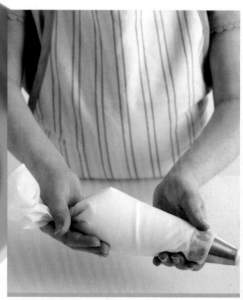

5 Transfer the meringue to a piping bag with a large nozzle.

Squeeze from the top

6 Pipe baskets of meringue on the baking parchment using your circles as guides.

7 Bake the baskets for 1 to 1½ hours until the meringue is crisp on the outside and pale gold in colour. Turn off the oven. Leave the meringues in the oven until they are completely cold, preferably overnight.

☆ **Annabel's Tip**
If you don't want to pipe the meringue, spoon it onto the parchment and shape it with the back of the spoon.

Whisk the cream to soft peaks and spoon on top of the meringue

Decorate with mixed berries

Easy berry ice cream

This fresh, fruity ice cream is packed with berries. And you don't need an ice-cream machine to make it!

☆Annabel's Tip
If the ice cream is frozen solid, leave it in the fridge for 30 to 40 minutes to soften before serving.

You will need:
450 g (1 lb) strawberries
225 g (7½ oz) raspberries
225 g (7½ oz) blackberries
150 g (5½ oz) caster sugar
150 ml (5½ fl oz) double cream
1 to 3 tbsp icing sugar

1 Wash your fruit, pick out any bits of stalk, and hull the strawberries.

2 Put fruit and sugar in a pan, cover, and cook slowly for 5 to 10 minutes.

3 When the berries let out their juice, turn up the heat and simmer for 5 minutes.

4 Let the fruit cool, then blend it until it's smooth.

5 Pour the blended fruit through a sieve to remove the seeds.

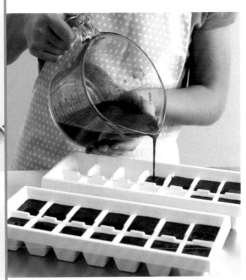

6 Pour the sieved fruit into ice-cube trays and freeze until solid.

7 Put the cream in a bowl and whip it until it forms soft peaks when you lift the whisk.

8 Let the frozen berries thaw for 5 minutes, then roughly chop in a food processor. Add the cream.

9 Whizz to combine, then add icing sugar to taste. Serve now (it is quite soft), or freeze for an hour before serving.

Techniques

Learning basic cooking skills such as chopping, kneading, grilling, and griddling is the first step to becoming a good cook. So here's a simple step-by-step guide that will help you tackle most recipes and turn you into a superstar chef…

Preparing ingredients

After you've read through a recipe and got all the ingredients together, the fun can start. First you need to get everything ready – chop vegetables, grate cheese, prepare breadcrumbs, or make up stock. Then you can start cooking!

Chopping

Bridge technique
Hold the fruit or vegetable between the thumb and index finger of one hand. Hold the knife in the other hand and cut under the "bridge".

Claw technique
Hold the flat side of the ingredient on the chopping board. Hold your other hand in a claw shape to keep it steady. Move the "claw" along as you cut.

⚠ Always take extra care when using sharp knives or graters, or electrical equipment including cookers.

Dicing

1 Peel your onion and cut it in half.

2 Cut slices through in one direction, then slice at right angles to the first cuts. Cut across the slices to make cubes.

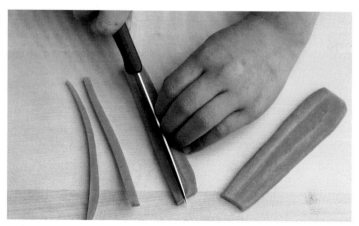

1 Peel your carrot. Then slice in one direction to make "planks". Cut the planks longways to make sticks.

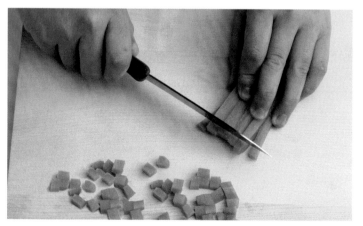

2 Hold the sticks to keep them steady, then cut them into dice. Try to keep the pieces roughly the same size.

Peeling

Hold a potato in one hand and a vegetable peeler in the other. Run the blade over the potato to peel off the skin. Always peel away from your body.

Use the same peeling technique on a carrot. You might find it easier to peel one end then turn it around and peel the other. Watch your fingers!

To peel a long strip of apple, start at the top and don't lift the peeler off the apple until you reach the bottom.

Grating

Zesting

Hold the grater firmly with one hand. Rub the cheese downwards over the teeth of the grater.

Use a grater with small teeth and small holes to grate ginger. Take care – wet foods can be slippery.

The zest of an orange or lemon is just the outside of the skin (not the white pith). Grate this off using a very fine-toothed grater.

Skinning a tomato

The skin slides off easily!

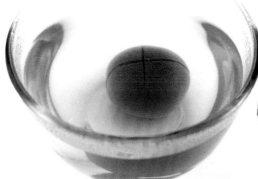

1 First cut a cross in the skin of the tomato.

2 Cover the tomato with hot water from a freshly boiled kettle. Leave for about 10 seconds.

3 Drain the tomato and put it in a bowl of cold water. When it's cool enough to handle, peel off the skin.

Making stock

Stir together

Vegetable

Chicken

Beef

Fish

Lamb

1 There are lots of ways to make stock, but here is how you make it from stock cubes.

2 Put a stock cube into a measuring jug and add hot water from the kettle (see packaging for how much water to use).

3 Stir until the stock cube has dissolved. That's it! The stock is now ready.

Making breadcrumbs

1 It is easiest to make breadcrumbs from bread that is several days old or slightly dried out.

Whizz it up!

2 Tear the bread into small pieces and put it in a food processor. Put on the lid and whizz.

Tip them out

3 In next-to-no-time your bread will turn into breadcrumbs. Now they're ready to use.

ALTERNATIVELY

If you don't have a food processor, use a grater instead. Simply rub the bread against the larger holes to make crumbs.

You can also buy ready-made breadcrumbs at the supermarket.

Flavouring

You can turn a dull dish into something really special without much effort at all! Here are some easy ways to add extra flavour.

Marinating

1 A marinade adds flavour to ingredients such as chicken. There are many different marinades, so make yours according to the recipe instructions.

2 Then all you do is pour the marinade over the meat. Leave it in the fridge for a few hours or overnight so the flavours can mingle.

When you're marinating meat, make sure it's completely covered. If the marinade is very acidic or salty, don't leave meat longer than 20 minutes.

Seasoning

Preparing garlic

Seasoning means adding salt and pepper to a dish. You don't need much of either – just a pinch of salt and a few grindings of pepper are usually enough.

1 Chop off the bottom of each garlic clove. To loosen the peel, crush the clove with the flat side of a knife.

2 To crush it, put the bare clove in a garlic crusher and squeeze the handles together.

Using herbs

"Soft" herbs such as mint, dill, basil, and parsley can be added at the end of cooking, but woody herbs like rosemary, lemongrass, and thyme are best added early on.

Lemongrass

Dill

Chives

Flat-leaf parsley

Mint

Basil

Coriander

Thyme

Curly parsley

Baking techniques

Baking is a real treat – I love all the beating, whisking, and kneading it involves, and I love the smell of freshly baked foods. But to be good at baking, you need to know the tricks of the trade. So here they are...

Creaming

⚠️

1 When you "cream" butter and sugar, you mix them together. It's easiest to do when the butter is at room temperature and quite soft. Start by cutting the butter into pieces.

2 Use an electric whisk or the back of a wooden spoon to squash and rub the butter into the sugar until everything is thoroughly combined, pale in colour, and light and fluffy.

Sifting

Folding in

This removes lumps and puts air into your mixture. Spoon flour into a sieve, hold over a bowl, and tap the sieve until all the flour falls through the holes.

1 This is a gentle way to stir in ingredients without knocking all the air out of a mixture. Use a spatula or metal spoon.

2 Run the spatula around the edge of the bowl, flat against the side. Then draw it across the middle with a cutting action, gently lifting the mixture as you go.

Beating

Hold the bowl in one hand and tip it slightly. Using a wooden spoon, stir the ingredients vigorously to make a smooth mixture and add air.

Separating an egg

1 First gently tap the egg on the side of a bowl to break the shell. Carefully pull the shell apart.

2 Tip the egg yolk from shell to shell, letting the egg white fall into a bowl. Put the yolk in another bowl.

Whisking egg whites

1 Put your egg whites into a clean bowl – if there is the tiniest bit of grease, the whites won't whisk properly. To be safe, wipe down bowl and beaters with paper towel dipped in lemon juice.

2 Whisk using an electric mixer or hand whisk. The whites will increase in volume as you whisk in air. They are ready when they stand in firm peaks.

If you over-whisk your egg whites, you will beat out the air and the egg whites will start to collapse.

Preparing a cake tin

1 First draw around your tin on baking paper. Cut enough paper to go up the sides of the tin.

2 Spread butter over the inside of the tin so the paper sticks.

3 Put the paper into the tin pencil-side down. Snip and fold the paper into each corner. Cut off any overhanging paper.

Rubbing in

1 This is a way to mix fat into flour. First put butter and flour into a bowl. If the butter isn't already cut up, cut the butter into the flour by chopping it into smaller pieces with a knife.

2 Pick up small handfuls with your fingertips. Rub your thumb along your fingertips letting the ingredients fall. Repeat until the mixture looks like fine breadcrumbs.

3 To check there are no large lumps of butter left, gently shake the bowl from side to side. The lumps will move to the surface and you can rub them in from there.

Kneading

1 This is part of bread making. First dust a surface with flour. Put your ball of dough on this. Then use the heel of your hand to squash and push the dough away from you.

2 Fold the top end of the dough towards you. Give the dough a quarter turn.

3 Repeat steps 1 and 2 until the dough is smooth and silky.

Ways of cooking

⚠ **TAKE CARE** All cooking should be done under adult supervision.

Recipes use different cooking methods to change the flavour and texture of a dish. Here's a glossary of the ones used in this book.

Boiling

When a liquid is boiling, it is bubbling vigorously.

Simmering

When a liquid is simmering, it is bubbling gently.

Pan frying

When you cook in a pan with a little oil you are pan frying or sautéing.

Stir-frying

Stir-frying is cooking in a frying pan or wok over a high heat, stirring constantly.

Grilling

Grilling is a way of cooking food under the heat of a grill.

Griddle cooking

Griddle pans heat up on the hob. Their raised ridges make food look barbecued.

Baking

Baking means to cook food in the oven. Cakes and biscuits are baked.

Roasting

When you cook vegetables, meat, or fish in a hot oven, you are roasting them.

Steaming

Steaming is cooking food in a steaming basket over a pan of boiling water.

Index

Annabel Karmel

Annabel Karmel is a best selling author on cooking for children and her books are published all over the world.

She is an expert in devising tasty and nutritious meals for children without the need to spend hours in the kitchen.

Annabel writes for many newspapers and magazines and appears frequently on radio and TV as one of the UK's experts on children's nutritional needs. She has her own range of healthy foods for children in supermarkets and a co-branded line of children's foods with Disney. She also produces a range of kids' cooking equipment.

Annabel was awarded an MBE in the 2006 Queen's Honours List for her outstanding work in the field of child nutrition.

Other children's titles written by Annabel
Children's First Cookbook   Cook It Together   Visit Annabel's website at
Mummy and Me Cookbook   **www.annabelkarmel.com**

Acknowledgements

With thanks from Annabel to: Caroline Stearns, Seiko Hatfield, Dave King, Rachael Foster, Rachael Grady, Mary Ling, Penny Smith, Jonathan Lloyd, Evelyn Etkind, Liz Beckett, **and children who appeared in the photographs** Chiara Alongi, Nicolas Alongi, Ruby Christian-Muldoon, Emma Johnson, George Leigh, Fiona Lock, Aliyah Reid, Jordan Robinson, Tom Stewart, and Vikram Garewal.

Picture credits: The publisher would like to thank the following for their kind permission to reproduce their photographs:
Key: a-above; b-below/bottom; c-centre; l-left; r-right; t-top)
Alamy Images: Foodfolio 8cr, 127bl; Nic Hamilton Photographic 127c; D. Hurst 8bl.
StockFood.com: K. Arras 79cb; Dave King 127cr; Peter Medilek 57crb.

All other images © Dorling Kindersley
For further information see: www.dkimages.com